SACRED MYST

'With ancestral Bardic tongue Finbarr cou
that illustrates the Way of the Initiate; the
into the liberation of body, mind and spir
Finbarr's telling of his personal inner pilg
and compassion for our shared suffering. Hand in hand with the Divine Mother,
whose counsel, 'KNOW THYSELF!' he takes to heart, Finbarr, a skilled and
caring guide, shows us that we, too, can trust, relax and lay our burdens down.'
Claire Heartsong *'Anna, Grandmother of Jesus' and 'Anna, the Voice of the Magdalenes' with*
Catherine Ann Clemett

'Sacred Mystical Journey is a compendium of life's learnings. Love's capacity to
transform us, and a deep and riveting account of the capacity to transmute betrayal
into forgiveness and adversity into blessing. Through Ross's honesty and
vulnerability we come to understand that each of us has the power to "love what
we have hated, to love what we feared, and to love what has haunted, or hurt us."
Using a map of spiritual principles, Ross shares with us an inner world of wisdom
that is our birthright, and brings us a tried and true formula for resolution and
ultimate absolution, through forgiveness, healing and love.'
Flo Aeveia Magdalena *'Remember Union' and 'Sunlight on Water'*

'It's not often when a story weaves together a harrowing real life hero's journey with
the discovery of profound sacred knowledge. In Sacred Mystical Journey Finbarr
Ross courageously shares his personal 'page-turning' life experiences and his sincere
quest for finding his own life purpose. How does one feel the true gift as well as
what is ours to offer in a place that appears bleak beyond our imagining? In the
spirit of The Alchemist the reader is guided to places normally not accessed, with
the opportunity to feel honest compassion for ourselves and others, while finding
healing, growth and love in the most unlikely of places. A worthwhile journey
indeed.'
Sunny Chayes *Host of ABC 'Solutionary Sundays' and 'Pioneers of Possibility' on*
Spanish/English Mindalia TV, Feature writer and Chief Strategist for Whole Life Times, Global Peace
and Environmental Activist.

'Truth is truth, but not all truth is your truth. You must find your truth and then you are responsible for it." This is one of my favorite quotes that was given to me by the Divine Mary Magdalene. As I read Finbarr Ross book Sacred Mystical Journey those words came alive within my heart even more deeply. Within the pages of this book the above words by Mary Magdalene will ring true for you as you embark on this very intimate journey with Finbarr as he finds his truths, and then becomes responsible for them. The courage, tenacity, faith and strength he endures as he places his trust in the divine that speaks to him and through him will move you. This is a sacred pilgrimage into the heart and spirit of a modern- day mystic who guides you on how to stand in the fire, and to believe that everything is in divine right order even in the most dire of circumstances. Finbarr's journey will empower you to trust and surrender each day to the prayer of "thy will, not my will, thy way not my way so you too can fulfill your soul's destiny and stand firmly in the truths that are yours and yours alone.'

Joan Clark *Author of the Mary Magdalene Daily Devotional and Mary Magdalene's Walk of the Resurrection.*

Being lost in the dark forests of life can be deeply disturbing, just as finding oneself in a paradise of pure spirituality can be enchanting, yet there is no more profound a virtue than discovering freedom whilst on the mystical path. Finbarr Ross's book does just that, for as one embarks on the immensely compelling nature of his odyssey, one truly begins a SACRED MYSTICAL JOURNEY as the book's title reveals. Initially one is wrapped by the Celtic mists of Cork, before being plummeted into a life drama of great loss, only to once again soar into the fulfilment of a dream, in the land of dreams the great USA. Finbarr's writing is richly compelling and I felt inexorably drawn to the rich pathos of his story, as once again his odyssey moves into an horrific judicial arrest that incarcerates him for long periods of time, as well as holding him in an internal jail of shame and guilt, before discovering mercy and the self-righteous desire for justice – all as a result of his complete lack of perfidy or guilt. Once vindicated this saga smacks of the epic stories of yore, except Finbarr continuously draws us into the soul-lessons learned on his extraordinary odyssey, and so we move back to the lyrical source of all love and all faith, back into the arms of the Divine Mother. This book is a must for any spiritual initiate!

Stewart Pearce – *Master of Voice, Sound Alchemist & Angelic Emissary*

Sacred Mystical Journey

A Life Journey From Tragedy to Triumph

FINBARR ROSS

WHITE OAK

www.sacredmysticaljourney.com

Montrose, Colorado 81402
Ireland/UK/US
719 641 6764
finbarr@sacredmysticaljourneys.com

design by Ranchor Prime

ISBN 978-1-8383222-2-9
First published in 2021 by White Oak
an imprint of Fitzrovia Press
Glastonbury BA6 8HF, UK

printed by 4edge Ltd
Essex SS5 4AD
typeset in Centaur 12 point on 15
printed on Munken Prmium Bookwove 80gsm

Dedication

This book is in memory of my dear friend Dr. Jack Moriarty, a man with a heart as big as the planet who was always there for me both as a friend and as a mentor.

CONTENTS

FOREWORD

by Dr Sue Morter

I first met Finbarr Ross several years ago as he was helping me design a sacred site tour for a group of my students. Within a few moments, I knew I had found more than a tour guide, I'd found a soul friend. I know you have too, by finding this book.

Sacred Mystical Journey is not only a wealth of information, but it is wisdom disseminated through the alchemy of the Soul. It is eternal truth distilled through human struggle, pain and disillusionment into triumphant remembrance of our true nature as the Divine.

Having had an exalted spiritual awakening more than twenty years ago and being catapulted into a new reality because of it, I too have had the experience of the great walk of courage that is required to no longer be compelled through life hungry for acceptance and belonging and rather to be projected into flight and at one with the source of life itself. A life of fulfillment and grand adventure replaces the confinement of the False Self and its litany of needs. Life becomes truly a magical journey each day. Examples of how that looks within the human experience are the teachings within the pages you hold in your hands.

I was raised in a wholistic environment celebrating the body, mind, and spirit's ability to heal and rejuvenate anything and everything. Quantum science was the dinner table conversation as far back as I can remember. Energy Medicine is the only medicine I have ever required to live a robustly healthy life; it is what I have turned to every time I've encountered a challenge of injury, discomfort or complication of any sort. I've never gone to the doctor and taken an antibiotic to heal an ailment of any sort. As a doctor, I've treated and taught tens of thousands of patients and clients over the past 35 years and spoken to audiences all over the world on topics of enlightenment and embodiment, healing and wholeness, life and the after-life. In those experiences I have tied together quantum science, spirituality and human potential and aimed recipients' focus at full empowerment beyond the limitations of living as a believing machine. I've attempted to awaken humanity to their true nature beyond their analytical, educated minds. Many thousands of people have healed in this process. I personally am included in this blessed group of people who have awakened to our power to heal – to more than heal – to create. I healed migraine headaches so debilitating I would miss work in my own clinic one or two days per week for months on end, healed a scoliosis in my spine, and a deep fear of vulnerability and intimacy stemming from abuse in my early life as a child. I did so through the concepts that Finbarr speaks of here. I healed and I know you can as well. All we need do is remember who we truly are. The stories of those who have tied these concepts together and lived into them, are a source of guidance and inspiration.

Ultimately I know that you can heal as you read these words and implement them, because what Sacred Mystical Journey opens for you is the gateway to your own True Self, a Self where nothing seems broken, missing or wrong, but rather the version of you that knows its place in the cosmos as the creative power that animates source itself. Within this journey you will realize that you are the power of transformation packed into a body and as you activate the energies the Finbarr illuminates, they will rise in your life as a presence, cultivating a way of being that that transcends the mundane and illuminates possibility. You'll become inspired again. Your life experience will change.

I spoke in my book The Energy Codes: The Seven Step System for Awakening Your Life, Healing Your Body and Living Your Best Life about the necessity for awakening to a higher level of consciousness and living from there in order to authentically heal on every level of our lives. Finbarr speaks to this same necessity through his teachings of the Golden Flame of illumination and transmutation. He beautifully walks us through how to look into the eyes of life and see what it is offering us to heal ourselves rather than be suppressed by its appearances at first glance.

The universe is always functioning in our favor, if we choose to allow it. In fact, our life journey is to discover that truth and utilize it for our empowerment. We need only to discover how. My research has been shared in TED Talks, medical schools, talk shows and some of the largest spiritual centers in the world. I teach students in my workshops how to activate a higher level of awareness in their lives and how to build the neurocircuitry to sustain greater capacity to lead, love and create the life we can imagine. I teach them how to heal themselves. Finbarr offers you a healing path here as well with the words he uses and the manner in which he sees and shares his wisdom. He is truly an old soul and is here to give of his long lineage of insight and connection to the Divine. He is here in service; it is his calling.

There has never been a more important time to find the guidance that will propel us as individuals into our own magnificence. We are being led into an era of enlightenment and empowerment like we have not seen in our lifetime. It is imperative that we embrace this moment with clarity, strength and love. And while oftentimes love does not seem possible when we are steeped in fear and confusion, we are here to dispel the illusion that these perceptions have power over our ability to choose. In the final stages of awakening we realize that our own personal journey is the greatest teacher we will find. We discover that awakening in our own authentic manner at our personal pace is the greatest integrator of all. Loving ourselves enough to go our own way and allowing ourselves our own divine timing, ensures that we can never be compromised and ignites the creator within.

At this time the energetic frequencies of fear and confusion are surfacing in monumental proportion. This too is perfect. For centuries this friction has consistently been at the frontier of consciousness. By the turn of each century we discuss what challenges have unfolded and what we have accomplished in terms of rising to the call. Our current times are no different.

We are being beckoned into our greatness and as evolution would have it, we must learn new tools and expose ourselves to new languages that can reveal the next new path with ease and grace. Finbarr provides many ways to further your own magical journey by leaning into the ancient and immovable truths of a life based in the sacred. While some of the ideas may be new to you, the foundation beneath these words is tried and true, and can be found in the oldest of texts known to humanity. You are on a beautiful and right path to find yourself here, now.

Finbarr's stories from his personal life experience will help you carve a path of understanding for your own life experience, and while my research has resulted in information inspiring me to teach humanity to transcend their "story" and work with the raw energy of the universe that flows through the human body to heal and transform their lives, his accessible manner and love of life that expresses so meaningfully, will offer transformation in another form. It will show you that your own life journey, in the form of your "story" is a sacred one. In every way imaginable, we are here to bring the light of the highest into human consciousness. We do so when we feel afraid and internally choose to be soothed, when we are angry and choose to see that our anger is our own and is not caused by another, and when we realize that we can turn to one another, open our hearts, and collectively generate a different reality because we care more than we fear. It is through our own sacred, mystical journey that we transform. When we become curious, we turn our journey into something sacred. When we work together, we are more; we are closer to true Oneness, where the Soul can thrive.

It is my sense that your life will thrive more because you have met a new soul friend in Finbarr Ross, and that you will be deeply moved by his life's work and through this beautiful orchestration of his love for humanity here, in Sacred Mystical Journey.

Dr. Sue Morter
Founder, Morter Institute for BioEnergetics
Best Selling author of The Energy Codes: The 7 Step System to Awaken Your Spirit, Heal Your Body and Live Your Best Life

What do we learn from tragedy?

Being connected to the human experience—whether tragic or exuberant—
can make us feel alive and drive us to lessen the suffering of others. If we
are in tune with others and able to step outside of ourselves, tragedy can
be a magnificent wake up call, a loud reminder
to live authentic, meaningful lives.

MY WISH FOR YOU

We all have a story and this is mine. My desire for sharing it with you is to encourage you to trust that there is a benevolent power that is always watching over you even when you feel lost, alone, abandoned, full of despair and hopeless, know that you are not alone. On my walk from incarceration to illumination/spiritual awakening, my soul took me on a vision quest to meet myself. It was not easy as you will read in the pages that follow, but each step of the way has lead me to the life that my spirit was calling me to. Each experience tested me and grew me into the person I am proud to be today. My hope is that as you traverse through the pages of this book that you will be encouraged to trust more deeply that everything is in divine right order and that you are loved even when you feel like your life is falling apart. If you can, have even a seedling of faith that perhaps something is unfolding on your behalf for your highest good, something that has not been revealed to you yet, I promise life can take unexpected changes you could never even dream of…for the better. As you will see in the chapters that follow my life is living proof of it and I wish that for you as well.

NOVA SCOTIA 2019
—LOOKING BACK

"I was a listener in the woods. I was a gazer at stars." These are the words of Cormac, high king of Tara, but they are true of me as well. I am not a high king of Tara nor am I even descended from one. I am the son of a farmer. Being the son of a farmer I had no golden chariot, no winged horse, no magic cloak to convey me from the stench of manure, the smell of the bog, the cries of my brothers and sisters. Instead I had a bicycle, but that was later. In the beginning there was not even a bicycle, there was only work, work, and more work. I was the second child and a first born son to my parents. We lived on a farm, one of many that lay in the wild countryside that surrounded Dunmanway, a small town in the geographic heart of West Cork, Ireland. I was born during the last days of summer, the last days of World War II, the last days of a time and a place which no longer exists except in my memory. I see long lonely roads overgrown with wild fuchsia hedges, rhododendrons and wild roses. There are moments when I think about my mother in her apron, bent over a thick slab of dough from which she will fashion the crust of a gooseberry or apple pie, moments when I think about the light fading over the mountains. There are moments when I imagine I might make myself a little hermit's hut full of fallen ash branches and great green fronds of fern as I used to do when I was a child. Now there are moments when I think about being there but not of returning there. From the start my story was never about looking back, it was always about looking ahead. Yet there comes a time when you can no longer look ahead without looking back and for me that time is now. In Irish folklore there is a story of a wise old man explaining the stages of life to a young boy. "You see, my boy," says the old man, "a man's life naturally divides itself into three distinct periods. The first, is that when he is planning and contriving all sorts of villainy and rascality; that is the period of youth and innocence." "The second is that in which he is putting into practice the villainy and rascality he contrived before; that is the prime of life or the flower of manhood." "The third period is that in which he is making his soul and preparing for another world; that is the period of dotage." I suppose my boyhood dreams of escaping my father's farm were a type of villainy and rascality in themselves. And later, in the flower of my manhood, there would be those who would accuse me of contriving to put such villainy and rascality into practice. As is true for all of us, the visions of childhood are shadows of things to come; but like the shadows in Plato's cave, most of us cannot truly distinguish between what is real and what our minds tell us reality is. As for the last, I hardly think that I am in my dotage, but perhaps there is truth in the notion of my preparing for another world. Yes, I am in the business of knowing my soul and preparing for another world...a world not separate and distinct from this one. A world inexplicably linked and interwoven with this one...like the strands of memory from which we weave our stories.

A memory; a story; a world.

For better or worse, this is mine.

INTRODUCTION

We have all been incarcerated. Growing up and living in society as we have known it, means along the way, we've all been imprisoned by limiting belief systems of some sort concerning abundance, health issues, family dynamics, self-esteem, worthiness, our achievements or any number of other perceived limitations. Walking the Mystical Path from Incarceration to Spiritual Awakening is the process of overcoming this imprisonment, whatever that is for you. Whether it is metaphorical or literal in my case, this journey of awakening brings you into not only freedom but a greater sense and understanding of who you are. It is 2007 and I am in Scotland on the Isle of Iona, standing in one of my favourite places, the Iona Abbey. Originally called the Isle of the Druids, I am at home here. I am with a group of seekers in this sacred space, experiencing the beauty and power of this most mystical place. Not everyone who comes here can feel the energy as it passes through their bodies without it leaving

7

a trace. However there are always those who will feel a tingling or will even be brought to tears as all will be affected in one way or another, sooner or later. Whether they know it or not, mists of wisdom of the Ancients swirl around them.

I am curious to see how this fledgling group of seekers will be affected. Noticing as each one finds their own energy spot, my eyes are pulled to a window at the very front, far to the right as the light streaming through it draws me like a moth to a flame. Standing in front of the window I feel the rays of the sun shining on my face as while closing my eyes reverently, I melt into the feeling. Gradually I become aware of the presence of Mother Mary. She shares a simple message with me.

"Are you aware that you agreed to be here, at this time, to bring forth the new dispensation starting on the winter solstice of this year? We are entering a five-year period of transparency. As such, 2008 will be the beginning, a fitting year for transparency."

Little did I realize that this was to be the beginning of a series of messages which were to come forth each year. A year or so ahead of time, I would receive a message from Mother Mary with information pertaining to the following year. When I receive a message, I ask for confirmation and it comes in many different forms. Sometimes I hear something on the radio or on television. I might pick up a book and it opens to a certain page or perhaps, I might hear a snippet of a conversation as I pass someone on the street and although the conduit differs the confirmation always comes forth. This time my confirmation came at Rosslyn Chapel in Scotland a few days later. Rosslyn Chapel is an awe-inspiring 'book in stone' whose builders were surely guided by the Ancients. I led the group to a particular power spot then I left them and went to another power point so they could have their experiences in their own favourite spots. At this other spot I became aware of a lady walking towards me who was not a member of our group. She was about fifty year's old, medium height, with dark hair and she appeared nervous as she addressed me, "Can I speak with you?" I thought to myself, "Oh God, what am I going to hear now?" Of course the courteous thing to do was to say yes to her. She surprised me by saying, "I have been asked to give you a message, are you open to receiving it?" My ears perked up as I responded, "absolutely!" She then said to me in a very matter of fact voice she had received a message from spirit to tell me, that we were here because we had agreed to be here at this time and that our mission was to bring forth the new dispensation. She repeated to me the same message I had received myself, almost word for word. She asked me if I understood its meaning, I said yes. We chatted for a few minutes and she told me how afraid she was of approaching a perfect stranger with a message that to some would sound like the ravings of a lunatic, but in the end the impulse to speak it was too strong to ignore. Thankfully she listened and mustered the courage to approach me. When she left, I thought, okay, this is it; I have my confirmation, now it was up to me. While I contemplated the enormity of the task I also felt calm as I realized everything which has happened in my life thus far has brought me to this point and prepared me for this task. Pondering over my life, I realized all the challenges which I've experienced were just as necessary and important as all of the blessings. In fact, in many ways, I recognized the challenges were also blessings.

Reflecting on this, I began to follow the threads of destiny throughout my life and I was brought right back to my childhood at about ten years old. I now realized that I did have mystical experiences even then which I didn't understand as I had no one to talk to about them or to explain things to me. I became fully aware that this was when the seeds of my future began to germinate, that these were the seeds of my awakening. However the seeds of my awakening didn't start out all joyful and rosy, it was quite the opposite really. May my story inspire you and help you in your own awakening.

I AM the light that I AM

I AM the peace that I AM

I AM the love that I AM

I AM the Christ of God, I am That I AM

PART ONE

CRACKING OPEN
THE EGO

✼

1

MY BACKGROUND

We all come into this life with the seeds of our gifts ready to germinate. These seeds are moulded by our environment, our circumstances and the people in our lives. Often in order to have the seeds germinate and grow into our gifts which we can share with others, just as with nuts from a tree, the hard shell needs to be broken to release the seed. In the case of human beings this is often accomplished by the unintended cracking open of our ego. These are the circumstances, challenges, and the seeming victimization we experience in life which often prompts us to start our spiritual journey of going within to find answers. Before I tell you what occurred when I was ten, I think I should give you an idea of my background and who my family were as the people who shaped me, moulded me and gave me a sense of who I was.

I was named George Finbarr, but nobody called me George, everybody called me Finbarr. Finbarr was a Saint, but so was

George, in fact, everyone in my town in West Cork, Ireland was named for a saint. Well, actually everyone was named for a grandfather or a grandmother but all the grandfathers and grandmothers were named for saints, so in the end everyone was named for a saint. There was a reason for this, Saints were holy people and they could endure all of life's challenges because of their love for God. I wondered what it would feel like to love something or someone so fiercely. This kind of love intrigued me. I wondered why it was that only Catholics became a saint. No one ever heard of Protestant saints and I wondered why, because my grandfather was Protestant. It made me wonder how they were different from Catholics as I couldn't see any differences when I went to visit my relatives, cousins who were both Catholic and Protestant. So what was it? It seemed to me there wasn't any difference at all.

I was a curious child with a lot of questions, way too many in fact. I had been told over and over to; "Never mind why, just do as you are told!" and these words rang in my ears time and time again. Still, sometimes my older sister Anne would pass me bits of information like when I asked her where babies came from she told me that they were found under cabbage leaves. I spent some time wondering how they could come from a head of cabbage especially when there was frost on the ground: this question was prompted by the arrival of my twin sisters. I also had other questions related to that but my sister wouldn't answer them. I certainly couldn't ask my father about any of these things as he had no patience for questions and very little for me. Until a few years ago, I couldn't understand why and as a child I felt only hurt. He was a hard man, devoid of emotion. He could devastate you with the lash of his tongue and then crush you with his anger.

2

MY FATHER

he wasn't a big man at just short of five foot nine but he was lean and hard like a boxer. He never gained or lost a pound that anyone could tell which was surprising because his appetite was enormous: he loved his food and it was over food that our first battles began. He enjoyed his bacon and ham and as we lived on a farm, surrounded by cattle, sheep and pigs, we always had thick slabs of meat to eat, usually pork or lamb. He couldn't understand why I wouldn't eat bacon, my mother ate it so why couldn't I. Somehow she knew my stomach turned whenever I looked at the pink flesh surrounded by the fat. She tried to spare me by serving me the thinnest and leanest pieces she could find, but there were times when I simply couldn't swallow even the tiniest bit. This would trigger the familiar battle of wills between my father and I as he would stare me straight in the eyes and then stare at the plate before me. I would stare straight back: I was not physically afraid of him as I was certain he would not hit me. "You do not know what is good for you boy!" he bellowed.

When this happened, I knew I could not look away, somehow that would mean defeat so I continued to stare back. He glared back at me intently, his eyes filled with the same aversion and loathing toward me which I felt for the streaky bacon. I didn't understand why he disliked me or why I felt I needed to fight back so strongly, I only knew that if I wanted to survive, I could not let him overpower me. When he realized I wouldn't back down, without taking his eyes off my face, he would mutter with disdain, "You're son woman, you're son woman!" I would not let him know how deeply his words hurt me and as time went by; the wounds went deeper and became more infectious than any blow from the back of his hand would have been.

Being the eldest boy only added to the friction between my father and I as there were additional levels of responsibility which came with that position. I was expected to know how to light the gas lamps, help care for the livestock, tend the vegetables in the garden, how to grow the different fruits, milk the cows, clean the barns and shovel the manure. I had to keep track of my younger brothers and sisters and make sure they washed up as well. There was also the clearing of the stones from the fields, fetching water from the well, and knowing just the right way to lift the heavy kettle off the fire and so many more things. I tried so hard, I did my best, but in the end I knew it just wouldn't be enough. My father would inevitably be standing there, scowling and shaking his head in disgust: "uscless!" he'd say, "absolutely useless!"

When things got really bad I would look at the road in front of the house wishing it could take me far away to Dublin or even further. In my daydreams that road was my escape route. I

17

did however find a place to hide from the realities of the day which was in the woods. I would go there to escape and to think: I felt safe there. The woods welcomed me and even spoke or sang to me on occasion, that was the way of the woods. After a while I built myself a little hut, it wasn't grand, but it was mine, it was a place I could disappear into where I could sit and fathom things out. I used dead tree branches to fashion the walls by intertwining them vertically and horizontally. I made the roof by layering huge fern leaves over the branches, laying them one upon another. I swept the dirt floor of all the rocks and laid ferns down for flooring. Another layer of ferns served as my door and I would crawl inside pulling the ferns closed behind me, there was no one who could find me in there. Other times I would roam the woods with a huge walking stick in my hand, fancying myself as an explorer of the great wide world. I'd climb a tree and watch all that I could survey. I'd listen to the frogs croaking and stare at the clouds as they raced overhead and disappeared behind the sun. Being in the woods was more than just an escape for me, it was where I felt most myself and where my imagination brought me to magical places. It was no wonder I would lose all track of time and be late in returning home, only to face the wrath of my father. He would comment, to no one in particular, about how selfish and lazy a thing I was to wander in from who knows where, doing who knows what, when decent honest people still had a hard day's work to be done and I could feel the anger rising like flames in my cheeks. Why did he have to ruin everything? I wanted to make him understand how I felt when I was in the woods but it was pointless. I was too young to put words to it. Talking about bluebells, I intuitively knew he had no soul to feel it: his outlook on existence reflected that. "Life is tough, boy," he'd say, "life is tough!"

He wasn't the only one to say that. My teachers repeated that and so did the nuns and priests. I didn't need to be told, everywhere I looked I could see that. In my hut I would daydream of taking to the road and escaping the life I knew. Now, looking back, I wonder what made my father the way he was as I don't know much about his childhood. I have no idea what his parents were like or anything about my ancestors or my own history as he didn't talk of such things. It seemed that all his energy, and ours, was consumed with the farm and with its endless chores; the cows and pigs that had to be fed, the cows that had to be milked and the stalls that had to be mucked out in the winter. The little I do know about my father is that he and his brother William left home as teenagers, turning their backs on their father and his new wife who had never treated them well. They both walked away never looking back. My father's mother died when he was three years old and the woman who took her place had neither the time nor inclination for mothering her stepchildren as she had her own children to mother. So it was that Nathaniel Ross took to the road one day with his brother William ending up settling ten miles down the road in the wilderness of West Cork where my father grew into a dry, selfish man, maybe growing up without a loving mother had something to do with that. Still, if only he could have done things differently, I might not have grown up without a loving father. In contrast, my Uncle William became a very different type of man, one who was kind, gentle and loving. I wish my father had been so, nevertheless, because of him, I developed a steely reserve that would serve me well thirty years later.

3

MY MOTHER

I knew a bit more about my mother's family as they were kind, caring and very connected to each other. My mother was quiet and gentle, the youngest of six children. Her connection to the Divine Mother was strong and she was known for her healing abilities. When people had ringworm even the doctors would send their patients to my mother because they knew the healing would be quicker. She would also intuitively know things as in one instance; for example, she got up in the morning informing us a telegram would be arriving. During the night she was awakened by hearing three knocks on the wall which was an indication to her of someone passing over so she would get out of bed and pray for them. The telegram arrived later that day letting us know that someone had died. This ability of my mother's was natural to us. Even though she worked hard on the farm, everyone knew that on Saturday afternoons my mother was not to be disturbed between 3:00 to 4:30. This time was reserved for one of her cousins who would arrive with coffee cake in hand. On Sundays our home seemed to be a stopping-off place for her brothers and her Uncle Felix, who would show up with his black and white dogs. Sunday night was usually spent playing Whist and other such card games as the responsibilities of the farm were parked at the door on Sundays. On other days, she would break the routine of chores with little pranks on us when we were children. One of our chores was to carry the milk pails to the churn. As we would approach our mother while she was milking the cow, without warning she would squirt us with hot milk. She had a playful side and that was one of her gifts to me. Another of the gifts which I received came from one of her sisters, Mae. When Mae became a nun she took a new name, Theresa, so to us, she was Aunt Theresa. She wore a long black habit and a funny white hat that looked like it had wings. She liked to hear stories and she liked to tell them as well. The ones I liked best were the stories of "the Troubles", the euphemistic name for the Irish War of Independence 1919-1921. These stories were of events which happened a long time before any of us children were born. She told us about the Black and Tans, the police reinforcements who were sent to Ireland to support the British police force, the Royal Irish Constabulary which had been defeated at this time by the Irish rebels, and how most Irish people believed that they were English convicts who had been released from prison on condition that they go to Ireland and fight. The Black and Tans had a savage reputation for brutality and were responsible for the sacking and burning of Cork City in December 1920 and many other towns and villages throughout the south of Ireland; even today their name is still despised by whole swathes of the Irish people. Though I couldn't truly understand 'The Troubles' or why they came and how they went, I found it both thrilling and scary to listen to Aunt Theresa. She would tell stories of how she and my mother would cross the fields to go to Mass only to suddenly find themselves caught in the midst of a hail of gunfire. I tried to imagine my mother throwing herself down onto the damp and muddy earth with bullets soaring and whizzing above her head, but somehow I couldn't. But sitting beside Aunt Theresa in her black habit when she was telling me the stories made it easy for me to picture her swooping to the ground like a great black bird, enfolding the vast span of her wings about my mother and herself to protect them from the bullets. I loved her and I loved how she loved me and my Mom. There were many other such instances as well. I didn't ever, as a child, understand 'The Troubles' or why people would shoot one another dead over the ringing of bells.

Aunt Theresa said it was a time of great sorrow and that we mustn't ever forget it so that it wouldn't happen again. One day, as I passed the kitchen, I heard my mother and Aunt Theresa discussing something in hushed tones. I pressed myself tight against the stone of the wall, held my breath and strained to hear what they were saying. All I could make out was something about bad girls and the bad men who made them that way. I wondered what made a person bad. Was it just the way they were born? Could they change? I knew better than to ask my mother about such things, but later, as Aunt Theresa and I were picking blackberries, I asked her, "What is it that makes a person bad?" She looked at me, then up at the blue expanse of sky overhead, and then back to me, "Finbarr, there is no such thing as a bad person, there are only people who haven't yet found their good." Like most answers to my questions, this one only left me more confused. Now, looking back, teaching me this way was her gift to me. Those were not just words for her but principles which she lived by. She even ran a halfway house for girls in London and she referred to them as her girls and she loved them dearly. Like Theresa, my Uncle Joseph Collins, her brother, seemed to be a figure of great romance and adventure. He had been captured by the British and taken to prison where he refused to give them his real name. He was my hero and I wanted to be like him and like my Aunt Theresa too. I wanted to be brave and stand up for something, even if I didn't quite know what that something was. When I went through my 'troubles', I thought of him often, and called on his bravery and her attitude towards others so that I could stay positive and hopeful.

4

SCHOOL AND CHURCH

When I was seven I received my first communion and was moved from the convent school to the boys' school, St Patrick's. The building was cold even though there were peat fires in the classroom. We had to stuff paper into the holes in the wall to keep out the chill. In the winter I tried to keep my fingers warm but I couldn't. I would get chilblains (a painful inflammation of the blood vessels below the skin as a response to repeated exposure to cold) and my fingers and toes would become red and swollen. I had to wear bandages on them when they burst, they'd start to itch and then I was in trouble until I could get home and my mother could put some ointment on them. In the second grade my teacher was Miss Brainey, she had a ruler that she used to whack our fingers with for some supposed infraction. She wasn't the worst though. Mr Bob Paterson was the third and fourth grade teacher, a very sadistic man and it was my misfortune to have him as a teacher. He used dowels for a cane and brought a playpen into the school. Every time he broke a dowel on one of us he would cut another from the playpen. He took pleasure in grabbing us by an ear and turning it as he dragged us across the room screaming with pain as tears ran down our faces. He would look for excuses to cane us. I remember when I was called to the front once because I didn't answer a maths question correctly. I held out my left hand to receive the caning and he noticed the bandages. He asked for my right one and saw it was also covered. He wanted to know why they were wrapped. I explained about the chilblains, but he made me remove the bandages anyway, to prove it. That didn't deter him though. Instead, he beat me across the backs of my legs. Still, it was better than having my fingers beaten to the point of swelling. But school wasn't all bad, even though I had a difficult time learning the Irish language. That trial was easily offset by other more interesting subjects. I liked geography because I felt like I was traveling to each of the different areas. I was an adventurer. History enhanced those journeys because there were reports about heroes having battles in all of those countries and going on quests there, exploring and battling the unknown. It reminded me of the stories I read in the comics. It was through them that I made three very good friends, Michael Rourke, James McCarthy and Pat Byrne. We bonded over comics, which was our great love at that age. Every Saturday we would each select a different one as soon as they were on the stands and then we would circulate them among ourselves. They were the best thing God had ever given us and we spent many a happy hour in the worlds between the pages of those precious comics. But once the school day ended, I still had to go home to chores and my father. It didn't matter that my fingers were stiff and throbbing from the chilblains in the winter. I still had to muck out the animal stalls, day in and day out, and as usual, my father would watch. He was impossible to please. I was grateful for the days I got home from school and he was not there. Things got a little better later in the third year at St Patrick's. I was asked if I wanted to be an altar boy and I jumped at the chance of having a few extra hours of freedom. There only appeared to be one challenge to the proposition, being that I had to learn how to serve Mass in Latin but that was easily remedied however by the headmaster, Mr Hourihan. The church was huge and I loved being in it. I liked the feelings I would have in my head, stomach, and throat and on the back of my neck and spine when the incense was burning and wafting all around me, especially during High Mass or the Easter ceremonies. I delighted in the way the rays of the sun shone through the different shades and hues of the stained glass, colouring everything they touched. I even liked the sound of the Latin we chanted. It is no wonder that in this magical environment, at the age of ten, I had my first of many experiences of the other worlds. One minute I was standing to the right of the priest and the next I felt a surge of energies going through my body and I could sense a loving presence surrounding me. I had no idea what was going on but I knew that it was special. As I looked around at the other people, I was sure it was only happening to me. I realised I had to keep my mouth shut and not speak of this because if I did, my days as an altar boy would have been over. I would have been ostracized once again, this time for letting 'the devil' enter me. I knew that wasn't true and wished I

27

had someone to talk to about what happened, but I couldn't take the chance because I loved the liberty of being an altar boy and didn't want to lose it. Certainly we had a routine: we had to be in town early, by seven forty-five am to serve Mass and then in winter we had to go straight to school but during the summer months when school was closed, that was a different story. Once Mass was over, if I was lucky, opportunities to stay in town would appear, like serving at a wedding or a funeral. Also there were lots of Priests home from the missions and quite often I would stay till noon, serving Masses for the various visiting priests. After three years, my days as an altar boy ended and so did my time at St Patrick's. That was just as well, because Vatican two came along soon after and the Mass changed from Latin to English and for me it lost its mysticism. There were also no more high masses, meaning no more escapes from my father. Alongside the many other changes happening in my life, I also entered St Ronan's College, a secondary school. Not all of my friends moved on to there with me as some went on to boarding schools and others to the vocational school while others pursued different passions, like Gaelic football and hurling. I had no great interest in playing them but I did enjoy watching the sports from time to time. We had another great big bully for a teacher at St Ronan's College, Tom O' Reilly, who would kick us with his steel-tipped shoes if we were not writing fast enough on the board. He was a very nasty man and not just to me, there is one particular instance with this man that I will never forget. I was sitting in his Maths class one day, watching him filling the board with one of his endless equations that seemed to stretch itself across the vastness of the black universe, when he turned around with a cruel smile on his face and said, "I have a message for the tutini gang (the smokers). I am going to bring in an ash colagheen (an ash cane) and straighten you guys out." We all thought, there is no way he is going to do that! I watched him as he stood there, stuffed like a sausage into his tweed jacket, his eyes moving across the rows of desks, looking at each of us. He then abruptly, continued with the lesson. A couple of days later he called on Buckley to come up to the board to solve an equation. I watched this big kid walk up to the front and pick up the chalk. He was just starting to write the solution when, with the speed of lightning, O'Reilly was smashing around his head and face with an ash cane, over and over. Blood was flying across the room as O'Reilly continued to thrash Buckley, who was running towards the door. He was almost there but couldn't open the door because the door handle was on the left and O'Reilly had him trapped on the right, hitting him viciously. It was only when O'Reilly ran out of breath, panting from the exertion, that Buckley had an opportunity to grab the handle and get out. By then there was blood everywhere. As all of this was going on, I kept thinking, oh my God he'll never get out of the door! To this day I can still see Buckley cornered and Tomo beating him. I never saw Buckley again, or heard anything of him. But when I think of him and that incident I still feel my stomach churn. Tomo (Mr O'Reilly's nickname) was one of the most brutal teachers I ever encountered.

Besides him, I had to deal with passing the Intercert or the Intermediate Certification test required for entering the last two years of secondary school in Ireland and so I spent most of third year studying for that. In order to pass it, I had to ace every single subject, including Irish, which was the bane of my existence. With all of this going on, I was spending more and more time in my old haunt, the hut, as it was the one place where I felt safe. At home I had to deal with my father and the endless battles over food and the constant criticism over the chores I did. I was afraid and frustrated as well, because my father seemed to use me as a target to vent his anger and then turned it on anyone who was near me. My mother would subtly shake her head, pleading with me not to set him off, which was what he was after as then he would direct his anger at her as acid spewed out of his mouth. If I was working on the farm and the farm hand, Donald, was there, he would look at me, shake his head and ask me not to say anything when my father went into his tirade. Otherwise, he knew he would become the target, so I had to just take whatever my father dished out because I knew he would also turn on Donald, the hired hand. I was always on edge, never knowing what would set him off. I felt isolated and alone. No one could help me so I lived in constant fear, not just at home but at school too. I never knew when I would feel the ruler on my fingers or the cane on my hands. I hated my life. I couldn't wait to be old enough to take to the road and go to Dublin, but, at that time, my only escape was the hut, and it was there that I could shake off the horrors of my life. It was there that I would enter into another world. After the heightened experience I had at church, I found I could close my eyes and see images and colours. These images would morph and their colours would swirl and spin and shoot off into a kaleidoscope of hues. I would feel my body tingle in the same way it did when the bells rang at Mass and I felt like I never wanted to open my eyes again.

I didn't know how, or why, I could see these things, and I had no one to talk to about it, so I kept it to myself: again, I was isolated. All I had was my missal with one side of the page in Latin and the other in English. I searched it for answers but found none. In the end, I didn't pass the Inter cert exam and I had to leave school. Mr Dilworth, the Principal, noticed I was good with numbers and suggested I take a correspondence course in cost accounting as well as recommending a job for me after I completed my course with John Atkins and Company. It was in this office of the local millers and builder providers, where I learned to use my newfound skills. I found I was good at it and I also gained knowledge of a number of other things as well. I learned about tools, hardware, hay barns, and how to build things. One of my colleagues, Harry Love, encouraged me to join a rugby team and I loved the excitement of it, the clutching of the ball and running down the field away from someone trying to catch me. I also made new friends, mostly from West Cork. I really enjoyed going to the movies and to the dances every Sunday night with my friends because it was the only way to meet girls, though I never had a girlfriend until I moved to Dublin. That fair city was still always at the forefront of my mind because I still lived at home. The verbal battles with my father eased but were replaced by the silent treatment. That continued until the day I left for Dublin, four years later.

5

DUBLIN

The fires within my soul still burned with passion to live in Dublin. This desire was fuelled for many reasons all through my childhood and into my teens, but mostly by our Dublin visits to my Uncle Joe. Getting the job at Atkins brought me closer to my goal. I worked hard and learned everything I could. In the meantime I constantly watched the ads in the paper for jobs in Dublin. After a time I found one that I was qualified for, at a timber importers and merchants called T&C Martins. It was in the timber importing office on Dublin Docks. This ad appeared the same week that I had to go to Dublin for a rugby match so an interview was set up for that Saturday. I aced it and got the job. I was thrilled. Finally, after years and years of wishing and dreaming, I was able to take to the road which took me to the streets of Dublin. I was finally liberated! One of my previous colleagues put me in touch with his brother John who lived in Dublin. I found myself sharing a studio apartment with this quiet, lovely man who was a few years older than I. It was the most wonderful time of my life. I was a man now in charge of my own destiny and I was free. I loved Dublin and she loved me. I took great pleasure in walking her meandering streets as the everyday sounds of this magnificent city accompanied me. I loved the peace and tranquillity of my new home. I was free to come and go as I pleased. Never again did I have to worry as to what I would find when I got home. After three years with T&C Martin a friend of mine told me about a job coming up in Weatherwell, Building Merchants and manufacturers but the only problem was, I needed a car and I couldn't get a loan for the car without my father co-signing for it. He absolutely refused; I talked to my mother and she told me to phone back in an hour. When I did so, it was all arranged! I found out later that it was my good fortune only because my Uncle Willie was visiting my parents at the time. He emphatically told my father that if he wouldn't co-sign, that he, Willie, would! They basically blackmailed my father, who was furious. I didn't care. I got the car and I got the job.

They liked me and I liked them so I thrived there. I was on the road selling building supplies and had a territory that covered the six north-eastern counties of Ireland. I thoroughly enjoyed both the solitude of driving and the meeting of new people but life had other plans for me. Three months after I started working there, the company was bought by their leading competitor, Gypsum. I was called up to the company headquarters one Friday afternoon and was told, effective immediately, that my services were no longer required and was then handed a white envelope containing my severance pay. My boss was kind enough to tell me that the matter was out of his hands. He gave me an enthusiastic reference and wished me good luck. It was a bad time to be out of a job. Any time was, but to be laid off in November was especially bad. In the winter months no one was hiring. It took me six weeks to find work and during that time I went through what little savings I had and got rid of my car. Finally I landed a job with Norwich Union Life Insurance Company. Initially I was hired as a fast-track trainee manager because I knew nothing about life insurance, which was exactly what they were looking for plus I was also a good salesman, which was the other thing they were looking for. They wanted to have people with no previous insurance experience, who hadn't been spoiled, who were people they could build from the ground up; I was one of their men. I joined nine other people for training in a small private hotel in the centre of Dublin just off Dame Street. Norwich was just initiating a new training program and we were the first guinea pigs. Instead of just putting us behind a desk, they decided they would try a new program that would fast-track the training process by providing five or six weeks of intense instructions and on the job training up front. They had never done this before; it was an experiment for Norwich. They were trying to impart knowledge usually gleaned over a two-year period of work into five or six weeks of training. Could it work? Absolutely! I was exposed to pension planning, life insurance, estate planning, investments, mortgages and annuities. I discovered I was especially attracted to the course on mortgages. The steps involved made perfect sense to me; the application process, the risk assessment, and the valuation. The sequence seemed to flow like poetry and to my delight I found I was a natural with it. Once that portion of our training was completed, we were sent to Norwich where the training was intensified. We were exposed to, and trained in, every aspect of the financial business of the company. As part of that we were shown the computer room where all the information was stored. This was a full room dedicated to monstrous machines, a room that seemed to stretch like an ocean liner across a sea of marble flooring. This was my first exposure to computers. It finally dawned on me that this company was much bigger than I had thought. I had a heavier workload than most college students did and I studied and worked twice as hard but finally we were done. Two of us were sent back to Dublin at the end of the two weeks while the others were scattered to offices all over the United Kingdom. I had come a long way from the farm and my days of mucking out the stalls and I was only twenty-two years old. The world was my oyster.

6

BERNADETTE

In the meantime, earlier in the year, I was at a trade show when I happened to spot a very nice-looking young lady. She had blue eyes, lovely long dark hair and a gorgeous figure. I was trying to think of a way to approach her when I noticed her slip was showing, just a wee bit. Great! I thought. "Hey lady!" I said. "Hey lady, you're slipping!" That beautiful girl turned to me, her face flushed with embarrassment. I don't remember how she responded, but she did. Although it might not have been the best pick-up line, it worked. I found out her name was Bernadette and our courtship began. I found her to be sweet and kind and I felt we were well matched. She must have thought so too, because two years later when I proposed, she accepted and I was a very happy man. We set the wedding date and planned to go to Spain for our honeymoon. Finally the day arrived, but unfortunately for us, it was snowing. Now, it isn't that it doesn't snow in Dublin, it does, but no one remembered it ever snowing as much as it did that day. Because of this, Bernadette and I spent our first night as man and wife stranded at Dublin Airport waiting to fly to Spain. It was not a great start, but finally we arrived in Spain. This was my first trip out of the British Isles and I was delighted to get off the plane and be greeted by the beautiful warm weather and sunshine. My senses were constantly bombarded by Latin music, laughter and loud conversations: I loved it. But this was in the time of Franco, the Spanish dictator who ruled the country. It was the first time I turned a corner in a plaza and saw a soldier carrying a gun, I was so shocked by this and they were patrolling on the beach as well. On the one hand it was nice to feel protected, but on the other, it was disconcerting. We certainly weren't in Dublin any more, that was for sure. As it turned out we wouldn't be back in Dublin for a few more years.

A few weeks before I got married I had been transferred to London so my new bride and I returned from our honeymoon to start our life together there. I worked in London from 1969 to 1972 as a consultant calling on bankers, investment consultants, insurance brokers, accountants and pension consultants. The work was great, but it was not a good time for an Irishman to be in London. The Troubles broke out again in Northern Ireland in 1969, over civil rights when the I.R.A., the Irish Republican Army, supported by many Catholics fought the protestant supporters of Britain who ruled Northern Ireland with the help of the British Army and from that point on, the hostility both within and without the office was extremely evident. One particular individual, Terry, had a problem with me from the very beginning. When I first started working there he commented on my pin-striped suit and asked where my pin-striped Wellingtons were. He would continue to make smart remarks about the Irish day-after-day until finally I had had enough. One night there had been a bombing in London and it was discovered that the ones responsible for the bombing were from Northern Ireland. The next morning he was making horrid remarks about the Irish and that was just it for me. I responded to him by saying, "Did something happen while I was sleeping last night? Because when I went to bed Northern Ireland was part of the United Kingdom. Did the United Kingdom cede it back to the Republic of Ireland during the night? If they didn't, then Northern Ireland is still part of the United Kingdom and it is a United Kingdom problem, not an Irish problem, so get your facts straight!" You could have heard a pin drop in the office. I never again heard another snide remark against the Irish. That was that. Still, I flourished within Norwich and it wasn't long before, at the age of twenty-three, I became the youngest person ever to become a consultant. At that time a salary was based on an age scale so it took the company over a year to determine what fair compensation was. I was doing the work of twenty-eight-year-olds: I was Norwich's success story. While the other trainees took two years to complete the program, I had completed it within a year. I was very fortunate to have some good mentors that also helped me along the way. They passed on the tricks of the trade, formulas and techniques that were closely guarded, but the other side of the coin was that Terry wasn't the only nasty piece of work there. Another Assistant Regional Manager was as prejudiced as anyone I'd ever met. He didn't like the Irish, or the Catholics, or the Jews or many others. He was a hard, cruel man who finally contributed to my leaving Norwich.

My wife was very unhappy in London and I had been offered

a job in Dublin which I was considering. I was going back and forth on whether to accept it when things came to a head with this manager and that was the tipping point. By the time Christmas came in 1972, we had moved back to Dublin where I became an investment consultant for Duggan Insurances. By January of 1973 I felt prepared enough to set up my own business and so I created The Family Building Society. After two years, towards the end of 1974, I had built its asset base to two million pounds and it later merged with the Educational Building Society. As successful as my business was, my personal life was a mess. By now I had three children and a lovely home in the Georgian village in Castleknock. However my wife had become a shrieking shrew, a control freak and the worst type of human being. I loved her but she couldn't seem to accept my love graciously. She could be so sweet and loving to me one minute, and then the next minute, turn around and curse the day she met me. One day I realized that I had, in effect, married my father, but she was so much worse. You can't keep hiding that kind of thing from the hired help. One day when my wife was out of earshot, Mrs Clark, our housekeeper, approached me: "Mr Ross, you can't keep living like this, Mr Ross, when are you going to do something about this?" She repeated it. "Mr Ross, you can't keep living like this!" she said as she shook her head sadly and I knew she was right. There was nothing I could do to make Bernadette happy and things were only getting worse. It began with Bernadette questioning me in the morning when I would leave for work, "What time will you be home?" "Six o'clock," I would answer. And when I arrived home at quarter to six she would glare at me. "You're a liar!" she would spit at me. "You said you would be home at six. You're nothing but a liar!" Every morning it was the same. "What time will you be home?" My answer was always, "Six o'clock." But life isn't that precise. If I arrived at ten past the hour she would glare at me. "You're a liar, Finbarr!" she would say. "You said you would be home at six. You're nothing but a liar!" It didn't matter what time I arrived home, quarter to six, six o'clock, ten past. I knew there was going to be trouble. It got so I hated even opening the door. I knew it was hopeless when after taking a shower one morning, I found the bathroom door locked from the outside. That became the new norm. She would keep me trapped there, screaming until I promised to give her whatever it was she wanted; more money, a new dress, a new pair of shoes, it could have been anything. Other times she would lock me in the living room so I couldn't leave for work. In those days keys were used for locking doors both from the inside and the outside and she had all the keys. I was a hostage until she got what she wanted but finally I figured a way out. I hid a key in the clock on the mantelpiece that would unlock the living-room window so I was able to make my getaway. I can still feel the thrill of that escape today, the pure pleasure of beating her at her own game. As I drove away I could see her standing at the front door with a look of surprise on her face. I waved with glee, but that was just one moment of triumph within years of abuse. The abuse continued: "Take me to that restaurant in town where you take your clients," she would say. "Bernadette, you know we can't afford that place," I'd say. She began to pace up and down the length of the hallway, back and forth, back and forth, as she thought of a response. "You'd bloody well take me there as if I were one of your precious clients!" she'd finally retort. "Yes, but if you were a client I'd be making a deal. The client would actually be paying for the dinner with the money I'd be making from his business." She couldn't argue with that, so instead, she'd scream: "You're nothing! You're useless and you're nothing! You're a cold, bloody bastard and I hate you!" And I'd stand there in my lovely house, in the lovely village, not too far from the banks of the River Liffey, wondering how the road could have brought me to where I now stood. Days later, when she had hurled something at me and ran out of the house screaming, I knew she would try to take off in the car. I knew when she was in that state of mind it wasn't safe for her to drive. I ran out quickly, but she was faster. She had gotten into the car, started the engine and locked the doors. All I could do was plant myself in front of the vehicle. I watched in amazement as my lovely wife, drove that lovely car, right into me. I was able to jump onto the bonnet of the car, clutching onto it and I watched her face as she drove up the road while my fingers were clinging to the bonnet, I was frantic. My young children were back at the house all alone. I thought, Dear God, how am I going to get off this car and get back to the children in one piece? My saving grace was that she had to stop before entering the main road. When she did, I jumped off and ran the quarter of a mile back to the house to my young children. When she finally returned I noticed there were dents on the right fender. She was hysterical and ranting, I called her doctor but he wasn't available so the locum doctor, a temporary replacement doctor when the regular doctor is away, came around instead. After seeing her, he came back to me, his face sombre. "Mr Ross, your wife has a serious condition and you really need to talk to Dr. McGuire on Monday. I have given her enough valium to knock out a horse but she is still wide awake. She is completely wired up; this is a serious condition, Mr Ross, a very serious condition." He didn't have to tell me that. I called Dr. McGuire only to be told that there was absolutely nothing wrong with my wife and that the locum doctor didn't know what he was talking about. He completely ignored anything I said and anything the locum reported. His suggestion was that I needed to work less and be home more. Other than being at work from eight-thirty until six, I was always home looking after the kids and the house. How much more could I do? The doctor ended by saying all she needed was a little break. When Bernadette heard that she decided she wanted to visit her sister and brother-in-law, so I took her to England to Maidenhead. During the visit she tried to stab me with a knife because I wouldn't extend our stay. I now realized I had to talk with someone about this so I called Oliver, a good friend of mine in Dublin, who also happened to be a lawyer as I thought he might be able to give me some advice as to what to do. I felt so ashamed having to tell him about everything, but I had to. I couldn't continue living with things the way they were. He didn't seem the least bit surprised as I gave him all the sordid details. "I know how bad it is," he said. "How could you possibly?" I asked. "You never met her." "Oh, but I have," he said. "I've met her twice." When did you meet her? "I asked. "I've called at the house twice when you were out," he responded. "She slammed the door in my face both times. She told me you had an office for business." "Why didn't you tell me this, Oliver?" "Finbarr, there wasn't any point." "If I could just make her happy then everything would be all right," I stated. "There's only one way to make her happy, Finbarr, but to do that you have to fathom out something." "What is it, Oliver? What do I have to fathom out?" "You have to fathom out that you are an individual with your own needs, too." I thanked him because I knew he was right. I suddenly saw everything in a new light. I had to learn how to make myself happy and until I did, I'd never be able to make her, or anyone else, happy. I was thirty-three years old, the father of three children and I had been trapped in a marriage for nine years. I had not known tenderness, nor physical passion, nor mutual respect during most of that time. I had been locked up in my own bathroom, had been hit by and driven on the bonnet of a car, had been almost hit on the side of the head with a bottle of wine, and had been stabbed at with a knife. With Mrs Clarke's words ringing in my ears, "Mr Ross, you need to do something, you cannot continue to live like this!" and Oliver's insight, I knew what I had to do next. It took me three months, but I finally left.

7

MY PROFESSIONAL LIFE

efore I left my marriage, in 1975, when I was still at home, I founded my second company, The Irish Investment Society. The time was right, I knew the economy was difficult, but I also knew there was a need for commercial mortgages for office buildings, warehouses and pubs. I also knew I could move a host of second mortgages because of the excellent return I could promise. By then I had learned not to rely on the middlemen, but I went directly to investors and would pitch fine-tuned offers, anything from six-month to five-year term deposits. I knew that service was the key to success so I would go out and visit my investors, which was something my competitors didn't do. The only thing was that I was bored with the more tedious aspects of property investments and the paper-work. Luckily, I met Frank Murray during one of my real estate transactions and worked with him for well over a year. I was impressed with the way he handled the detailed work which I so disliked. He had strong presentation skills and as a property fund manager, handled large portfolios so he seemed like a good fit. As fate would have it, he was looking to make a change in his life and career so I made him a partner and we became a formidable team. He ran the office and day-to-day operations. This gave me more time working the field bringing in investments and scouting new development projects. Our business was thriving and I had found my niche. Life was good. Then fate threw a wrench into the mix when the Republic of Ireland changed its disclosure laws which left me facing a difficult situation. Revenue authorities now required investment companies to provide detailed information regarding their investors. Many of my depositors came from the United Kingdom and Northern Ireland and they didn't want their names and addresses disclosed to the Irish revenue department. I had to figure out a way to keep them as clients in spite of the change in the disclosure laws. I knew there was a way. I just had to find it; and I did, in the form of George.

I had been on the search for a new accountant. A business associate, who was aware of this, introduced me to George. He was of medium height, a thin man in his thirties who had a boyish crop of strawberry blonde hair which constantly fell over his eyes. He was charismatic, easy-going and had an air of confidence about him which immediately made me feel at ease. I discussed my problem with him. "What you need to do is form an offshore company," said George. "I can make that happen for you. I've have all the contacts you need. Come to Gibraltar with me and we will get a special banking license there." "Will this give my investors and depositors the protection they need regarding the transfer of their monies?" I asked.

"Absolutely, Finbarr, trust me. We just have to go to 'The Rock'," said George. Gibraltar, I thought. The Pillar of Hercules, with its Cave of Saint Michael. It was connected to Saint Michael, Saint George and now to me, Finbarr Ross, and my newly formed company, International Investments Ltd. One of the requirements of securing the special license was that I needed a financial director that was a non-resident. Ronnie was someone I had met and worked with a few times in my business and even though he lived on the Isle of Man, he was willing to take on the role of Financial Director. Initially, he only provided services one week a month, but as the business grew, so did his contribution. My business continued to expand as I travelled to Belfast, London and the United States where we invested in commercial real estate, land, mortgages, leasing, as well as fine art, stocks and bonds, development projects, and gas and oil. It came at a price, though. I worked long hours and was always getting on a train or a plane to chase a contract. I pushed myself harder and harder to make more deals. I worried because I knew that raising a million pounds didn't mean I had a million pounds in my pocket. I worried because, more and more, the only people I spent time with, or talked with, were those with whom I was doing business. I worried because I started to think less and less about anything else. I told myself I was securing my future, and as such, my children's future, so that they would never have to know the pain and misery I had known along the road of life.

After my marriage dissolved, I only got to see them on the weekends, which was hard. They were looked after by a housekeeper. Still, I thought, some day, when I have closed enough deals, I would have the time to sit down with them and tell them how much I loved them and how hard I was working to secure their future; someday, one day soon. Then Bernadette threw me another surprise. One day I went to visit my children and my two younger ones were waiting for me, but I didn't see my eldest. "Where is he?" I asked Bernadette. "He's not here," she replied. "I can see that. Where is he then?" "He's gone away." "What do you mean, he's gone away? I asked, puzzled. "He's gone away to school. I've enrolled him in boarding-school. He needs discipline. He is out of control, just like you." "He's only seven years old!" I said, pain shooting through my body. "I am only thinking of him. I am only thinking of what is best for my son!" she spouted righteously. "You've done this to hurt me. You've done this to get even with me. That's why you've done this!" I retorted. "I've done what I've done because there's no one else to do it," she responded with satisfaction. I then entered a long drawn-out battle for legal custody of my children. While it was determined that I should have guardianship, the judge ruled that neither I, because I was a man and had a job, nor my dear wife, were suited to raise our children. At this time in Ireland there was no official family law. Each judge made up his own mind. There was no way a man in Ireland would be granted custody of his children because the belief was that men couldn't raise children. He ruled that the two younger children were to be left with my wife's sister in England and my eldest boy was to remain in boarding-school. I was totally shocked by the ruling. There was no appeal process. I felt absolutely violated and defeated. It took me a long time to come to terms with it and I had to find a way to cope. About ten years later I learned from a friend that the Barrister who represented Bernadette at the trail had had a moment of epiphany. Something in him awakened and made him realize that he could be ruining this man's life. He made himself a promise that he would not take on another family law case because he couldn't guarantee a fair outcome as there was no defined law for him to go by. He never again did take another family law case. My eldest son is now living in Washington State and my other son and daughter live in the United Kingdom.

8

SHEILA

My outlet for coping came to me through a friend, Arthur. "You have to do something, Finbarr; you have to find an outlet for all of this!" He played polo, so I joined him one day. I liked the rush and the power I felt sitting on that horse and spurring it forward using my long-handled mallet to drive the white wooden ball between the two poles. It was like playing rugby on horseback. I kept my ponies in the stables at Castleknock College. It was there that I met Sheila, a young woman who worked in the stables after school and full-time during the school holidays, where she was a riding instructor. She also taught German at Castleknock College. It was a simple process getting to know her because I could talk to her without having to take her to dinner. I could also ride with her without having to fall in love with her, but eventually it came to pass that I did both. We married in the quiet non-denominational University Church in London.

9

HOUSTON

In the meantime, in 1980 around Easter time, I went to New York to look at some real estate. I was supposed to meet a friend of mine there. When I arrived, my friend Austin mentioned he was thinking of taking a quick trip to Houston and he wondered if I would be interested in going along. At that time Houston was the fastest growing city in the United States and he was thinking of opening a restaurant there. I readily agreed. I loved it the minute I stepped off the airplane. A friend of Austin's showed us around Houston and for the next week we checked out potential locations for the restaurant and became familiar with the city. Austin found a location for his restaurant and I found a site for an office building and a joint venture partner in Houston for International Investments. In the autumn of 1980 Frank came to Houston with me and he really liked what he saw there. We ventured into it because of the vibrancy and glamor of the Houston market and over the next two years we made five investments in Houston. When I saw how successful we could be, in early 1983 I had a meeting with my partners, Frank and Ronnie. I was bubbling over with enthusiasm about the Houston investments and the unbelievable rate of their returns. I was surprised however at their lack of response. Both of them seemed distracted, indifferent and uncomfortable. "You're not really planning on staying in the States forever are you, Finbarr?" asks Ronnie? "I am thinking of it," I answered. "I like the people and I like the climate." Frank piped up with, "Finbarr, Ronnie and I have been talking quite a bit about the Houston investments. They're too far away for us. We feel we're better off concentrating our efforts here at home and in the United Kingdom. There's deals enough here." "Well," I countered, "I'm only doing what we've all agreed upon. We are already three years into the Houston investments. It's a bit late to back-pedal now, wouldn't you say?" Neither of them said a word. I knew their minds were already made up. I was blindsided. They didn't want to put any more money into America. "I'm committed to the States. It's no small investment we've made there," I said. "We know your visa has come through, we know you want to make your home in America. That's grand, really it is. We'd like to support you but we're not prepared to focus any more of our time or energy in Houston!" Ronnie firmly stated. In an instant I came up with a way out. "Well," I offered, "in that case, why don't I go ahead and follow through with my plans? I'll stay in America and oversee the investments we've made so far. As each property in the States is sold you'll get your share. When International Investments has all its money returned, then I'll turn full control of the company over to you. The bottom line is you'll get your money out of Houston. Once the returns are made, I'm through. I'll get myself out of

International Investments. The whole kit and caboodle will be yours to do with as you like." "Well, that's fine, Finbarr!" said Ronnie. "Fine indeed!" Frank agreed. "And clean," he added. We now had an exit strategy. I was free to move to the States and live there full-time. I was ready to but not my bride and I never saw it coming. I'd moved to the States and thought she was on board and excited to join me when her teaching for the school year finished, but when push came to shove and it was time for her to leave, she told me she had changed her mind. Her explanation was, "I am very close to my dada, Finbarr. I won't be leaving him so far behind. I can't do it." I was dumbfounded. With that, she was gone from my life. In hindsight, I realise there was more to the story. A couple of days after telling me she would not move with me, I asked her to pay a bill for me. I promised her my solicitor in Dublin would reimburse her within the week. She refused to pay the bill and told me that when money goes out the door, love goes out the window and that I could send her divorce papers and she would sign them. I was a single man again, bewildered and hurt. I simply couldn't fathom how a grown person could still be so influenced by their father. Maybe I could have stayed, but by then the die was cast and I had already committed myself to business dealings in Houston. Things had progressed too far and I couldn't back away, nor did I want to. So I returned to Houston full-time and focused vigorously on the investments there.

I sent International Investments a report each week via telex on the status of each of its investments. I talked with Frank a couple of times a month by phone and shared my information on the various projects. I no longer had any input or any real interest in the doings of the business in Ireland and the United Kingdom: my hands were full enough with the investments in the States, but I kept up my end of the bargain, scrupulously. I was a man of my word. As the autumn came that year, I decided I would go back to Ireland for Christmas. My children had been in my mind and I thought it would be good to see them. It would be a great Christmas, I thought. Not long after I made that decision, Frank called asking me if I would be in Ireland for the holidays. "Yes," I told him, "I will be. I'm planning to return about the middle of December to see my family." "Can you make it to Belfast on the fifteenth?" he requested. "What's in Belfast on the fifteenth?" I wondered aloud. "Our annual thank you luncheon for the investment brokers who will be there. I thought you might be willing to introduce me since I am in charge now. Although they know you, they don't all know me." "Sure, Frank I'll be there" I said. The day after I arrived in Dublin I took the train to Belfast with Frank, and then a cab through the leafy suburbs of the city to the elegant Stormont Hotel. As usual, the luncheon was a very friendly gathering where I introduced Frank. They knew of him and had dealt with him on the phone and such, but most had never met him. Frank then spoke and mentioned that he would now be fully responsible for running the company's affairs in Ireland and the United Kingdom. My role now was strictly working with our affairs in the United States. After the luncheon, we returned to Dublin, where Frank showed me a property that International Investments was attempting to acquire. It looked like a good investment to me and I said so. Frank was delighted with my assessment of the property. I then spent the holidays with my children and was a happy man. That New Year's Eve I looked back on all the trials and challenges I had faced, ones that were far behind me and thought, it is a new year and I am a new man, living a new life, in a new country. I was excited when I returned to the States to secure my future.

Back in Houston, later one evening in March, I returned home to see the red message light blinking on my answering machine. "Finbarr, its Ronnie. Frank and I are in town with some brokers from home. We're at the Grand Hotel. I've been trying to get in touch with you all day. Call me!" I felt something queer in my stomach. Something wasn't right. I returned his call, but the line rang and rang and rang. Finally he answered, his voice thick and heavy. "Hello?" "Ronnie? It's Finbarr. Are you ok? Hello? Ronnie, it's me. It's Finbarr. What are you doing in the States? Why didn't you call and tell me you were coming?" "Oh, hello Finbarr. Yes, yes I'm all right. I've taken a sleeping pill or two. I'm a bit tired at the moment." "Ronnie, what's going on? Your message sounded quite urgent." "We need to talk, Finbarr, but not now. I'm very tired." "First thing tomorrow morning then?" I asked. "Right," he responded. "Where?" "I'll meet you at Mama's Cafe at eighty-thirty. It's not far from the hotel. Grab a taxi, it won't take you but three minutes… Mama's café, Ronnie," I repeated. "Mama's Cafe at eight thirty." "Mama's Café," he mumbled. When he arrived at the cafe the next morning he looked worn out and haggard. He sat down at the table and lowered his head. He wouldn't look me in the eye. I waited for him to say something. Finally I hear, "We have a problem, Finbarr." "What sort of a problem, Ronnie?" "There's a bit of a problem with the cash flow at International." "What do you mean, a bit of a problem? What type of a problem, Ronnie? How much are we talking about here?" "Well it seems, Finbarr," he reported, "it seems that when Frank ran the cash flow projections, well, it seems that International Investments will be in a bit of cash flow bind in about three months or so." "It isn't possible, Ronnie," I stated. "Frank told me himself not two months ago that everything was in the black. How can it be possible that we are heading towards a cash flow crisis?" "Frank says we've some rather big maturities coming up at the end of April and May. As it stands now, we won't have the cash on hand to pay them, Finbarr." "Well, what else does Frank say, Ronnie? What else does he say about not having the cash? Has he taken into account the monies on deposit in Gibraltar, Newry and the Isle of Man?" "But that's the thing, Finbarr, he appears to have gone on a buying spree and not taken into account the maturities until now." I looked at him: I knew I should feel angry. I wanted to yell, "I thought you were there to make sure this didn't happen!" but I didn't. What was the point? Right now I needed to find a solution. Instead I said, "Right! Meet me in my office at eleven. Bring Frank and the other brokers, we'll sort this out then. Don't worry. We'll sort this all out!" As I left him, I thought, I should have known better. I should have seen this coming. I should have paid more attention to what was going on in Dublin. A few hours later, I sat behind my desk, in my office, and listened as Frank addressed Ronnie, me and the group of brokers from Belfast. "And in conclusion, I project we will be about two-hundred and fifty thousand pounds sterling short." He turned to me. "We need the cash, Finbarr. We need the cash and we need it now." "Are you asking me for money from our investments from here? You can't expect a penny from the Houston investments until at least six months from now," I explained. I felt my body start to tremble with anger. "Tell me, Frank, tell me please, how could this have happened?" I sat there shaking while Frank sheepishly admitted his own failure to keep up contact with the investors and brokers. It seemed things had come to a head when one of the brokers came forward with a withdrawal request of three-hundred-thousand pounds sterling. The ugly consequences of his neglect of these investors and brokers stared him in the face. There was nothing else he could say. Blame wouldn't save the day. We needed a solution. The five brokers in the meeting were eager to find a way to stave off the problem. The energy in the room shifted as we worked together to cobble together a deal that would secure International Investments. We determined that we needed eight-hundred and fifty-thousand pounds sterling. The brokers agreed to put up the cash. We calculated a new shareholder split allotment. The deal would take me out of the shareholding of International Investments and leave it all in the hands of Frank, Ronnie and the brokers. At this point I would have given anything to secure the company because I was still joined at the hip with them. I knew I only needed another year and a half to be completely independent of International. The cash flow problem was not a good thing, but it was something we could manage. I believed in Ronnie. Clearly it was Frank's mistakes that brought us to where we were. With the brokers on board and Ronnie in charge, I knew everything would turn out all right in the end. "What do you need me to do, Ronnie?" I asked. "I'll need your power of attorney. I'll need you to stay here and make sure the monies

we've got invested in the United States' projects are protected."
"If you'll have the letters drawn up? I will sign them." In a matter
of moments I handed over complete control of International
Investments to Ronnie, who then became a full partner. Frank
and Ronnie were named as co-managers and a few of the brokers
were selected to form a management committee to oversee the
operations. They left for Dublin with a basic plan in hand,
agreeing to meet again in three days' time there. All that was left
to do was for Ronnie to submit the changes of ownership to
our attorney in Gibraltar within the week and I would be out
of it. When they left I was drained. I had managed to find a
solution but I wondered how something like this could have ever
happened to me. The next few months were tense, but I managed
to keep the projects in the States on time and within budget.
The weekly reports from Frank indicated that everything was
progressing as it should at his end. But then in May the reports
stopped coming. I wondered what was happening. I heard there
was conflict between Ronnie and Frank and that the brokers had
not followed through with the promised infusion of cash. I tried
not to panic. Hang in there, I kept telling myself. Hang in there
and it will get worked out. You've been knocked down before
and have always been able to pick yourself up. Hang in there.
Push forward and don't look back. Whatever you do, don't look
back!

Then one hot and rainy July day, I received a telex from
Gibraltar Pillar of Hercules, from Ronnie, a very, very short one:
"Because of the situation, I have decided to put International
Investments into receivership today." Receivership is when an
outside entity, like an accounting firm, comes in to reorganise a

company that is facing financial difficulties. I kept staring at the telex in disbelief! I couldn't get a phone connection to Gibraltar to find out what was going on. Nothing made sense. I knew the investments of the company were worth so much more than the amount owed to the investors. When I finally reached Frank in Dublin, I voiced all my frustrations and fear into the phone. "Why did he do this? Why, Frank? Tell me why?" "Look, Finbarr. You gave him your power of attorney. " "Yes, I gave him my power of attorney. I gave him my power of attorney to protect the investments we have made! I gave him my power of attorney to protect our investors and to transfer ownership!" "Finbarr, you gave him the power! It was your choice!" When I tried to respond, he cut me off and just said, "Goodbye, Finbarr. Goodbye and good luck." With that he hung up. I was left standing there looking at the phone in my hand. Nine months later I was still in chaos. I had been working diligently to finish out the projects but I couldn't get the receiver's co-operation. Then Timothy Reville the receiver surreptitiously arrived from Gibraltar. He proceeded to visit all of our joint venture partners, contractors and bankers. He told them I no longer spoke for International Investments. He did this without my knowledge before letting me know that he was even in town. That was a big mistake. This supercilious Englishman knew nothing about business in the United States so he foolishly took a slash and burn approach. We were now dead in the water because none of the contractors or bankers were willing to continue doing business with us. All my personal money was tied up with the projects but the projects were now in limbo. I tried everything in my power to get the funds needed for the completion of one of them, the Mesa building. That one building alone would have been worth five million dollars if I could have pulled off the deal but Reville pretty well guaranteed that wouldn't happen. He was a petty man with a grudge against the Irish. He relished trying to ruin us and did the same in Dublin, I understand. He made bold statements about Oliver Conlon, my attorney, all of which were not true. He just went about things in such a way that it was impossible to succeed. Finally he was replaced by Gallanio, another receiver and I had to start from scratch again explaining everything. Finally, we reached an agreement which would have allowed me to complete some of the projects. A contract was drawn up, but once again, the receiver did not follow through on any of our agreements. I couldn't raise the last one hundred and twenty thousand dollars to cover interest and complete the building so tenants could move in. I never heard from anyone related to International Investments again. All the properties went into liquidation. Mike, one of our joint venture partners, filed for bankruptcy. With that, my house of cards fell down around me as banks started to call in the loans. Judgments were registered against me because of all the personal guarantees I had signed. Any money I would make from that day forward would be taken by one bank or another. From time to time my bank account would be cleaned out. I had lost everything.

10

PAMELA

ust as I was coming out the other end of this, Mike introduced me to Pamela. She was a fourth grade teacher with a lovely smile and a great sense of humour. She had long, fair hair and beautiful blue eyes, and as fate would have it, before I knew it I heard: "Do you, Finbarr, take this woman Pamela to have and to hold from this day forward? Do you promise to love and honour her above all others in sickness and in health, for better or worse, for richer or poorer until death do you part?" "I do," I said, and welcomed her and her two sons into my life. At the same time of my marriage I was laying plans to get my professional life back on track. Through a friend of mine I became aware of a position opening up in Dallas. I pursued it and ended up with a job offer to run a brokerage firm. The prerequisites were that I needed four different broker's licenses and had to become a member of the National Association of Securities Dealers (NASD), so I quickly enrolled at the University of Houston and signed up for the required courses. I took them in sequence over about a six-month period.

It was hard work but my training at Norwich held me in good stead and I passed with flying colours. I then became the managing partner, a title, which NASD gave to the person in charge of a brokerage house. That meant I had to commute over 200 miles from Houston to Dallas. Pamela was a teacher in Houston so I couldn't ask her to move. Instead, I would leave on Monday morning and return Friday evening. I did what I had to do. During the course of my job I did some business with a gentleman from the Philippines who was based in Geneva and so off I went to join him there while he and I worked on a joint venture project to raise several million dollars. I spent most of my time between Geneva and Vienna. However, I was still there a few months later trying to work out one last aspect of the deal. Christmas was coming up fast so I invited Pamela and the boys to join me there. I imagined a beautiful Christmas with them walking along the Danube, strolling through the Christmas markets. The day before Christmas Eve, Pamela phoned and told me she would not be coming to Vienna for Christmas after all as she had decided to go to visit her parents in Tyler, Texas, instead. A few days later she called again asking if I would be in the hotel on the morning of the 31st around 10:00am. I said, "Yes, I can be, why?" She informed me there would be a FedEx package arriving which would require a signature. I asked who it was from and what it was about. All she would only say it was from Ray Hardy who was a clerk of Harris County. And so it was that on New Year's Eve I received a sheaf of legal documents informing me that I was being served for divorce. I was forty-four years of age and had now had three wives. I thought Pamela was to be the last and didn't understand what had happened. I walked the streets alone watching as people passed by laughing. I looked at the Danube drifting lazily by and then walked down another side street leading me back to the darkness of my hotel room.

11

A NEW DOORWAY OPENS

I thought again about my past and my future and I knew there was more to life, that there must be a connection which I seemed to be missing. I went to church a few times a week looking for God, but I couldn't seem to get any answers there, either. When I returned from Vienna things got worse. I found out the brokerage was being sold and my services were no longer needed. Once again, I was without a job and without an income. I then started doing contract work for an agency as a market researcher, making good money. My heart wasn't in it though because anything I did make ended up in the pockets of the banks. I was looking for something more. Years after International Investments went into receivership, I was still paying the price for my own naïveté but still, I had to try. I began attending networking parties hoping to find a new job through someone there. It was at one of these that one particular lady approached me and introduced herself. "My name's Rebecca," she said, extending her hand. "Well I'm Finbarr, Finbarr Ross." Then she said, "Finbarr, do you dream?" That is exactly what this attractive and personable complete stranger asked me right after introducing herself. "Do you dream?" "No I don't. I just close my eyes and either watch a movie in my head or see a kaleidoscope of colours." Then she asked, "Do you meditate?" "No I don't...that's dangerous stuff. That's the stuff of brainwashing and the like," I responded. To my surprise, she laughed. Unsettled, I continued, "I'm quite serious. I've heard many stories about Scientology in Ireland about how they practice brainwashing through meditation." She laughed again, even more fully. "It's not at all funny," I declared. That was the beginning of many long discussions between us during which I learned about dreams and meditation and I was intrigued. She seemed to have the answers to many of my questions, questions I didn't even know I had until we talked. I found myself being drawn to the principles and the philosophies of her world. They made sense to me so I felt that I was in my element. She promised to take me through a guided meditation and a few nights later she did that at her home. When it was over, I thought all my birthdays had come at once. Some part of me felt I had finally found something I had been searching for years. It was lucky for me I lived so close because I left there with an armful of books about meditation, psychic development, esoteric teachings, theosophy and universal consciousness. When I read about Sophia, the Divine Feminine, and the Aquarian Rosary, something in me opened up and I immediately resonated with the information.

A little while later, one Sunday morning Rebecca introduced me to a group of people who met on a regular basis for spiritual discussions and so I joined them every Sunday and Wednesday whenever I was able to. I listened to a group of what appeared to be very normal, everyday people talk about their experiences with the Divine. I was blown away. Sundays usually entailed services and Wednesdays were filled with workshops. Joe Vaughan and his wife Nancy oversaw the teachings and meditations and they also offered counselling afterwards. I got to know them really well, in fact, Joe and I became good friends. He and Rebecca became my mentors as I walked this new path. I had a whole new lease on life. I was like a sponge eagerly absorbing everything I read. I also started to pray again, something I hadn't done since my days as an altar boy. I learned to pray the Aquarian Rosary, a Rosary practice which involves contemplating questions about oneself. In saying the rosary, every decket (a grouping of rosary beads with a certain phrase to contemplate), helped me look at issues in my life, to contemplate them and contemplate the road my life had taken. I would sit on my Zen bench and pray. Then I would find myself lying on the floor weeping tears of joy. I didn't understand what precipitated the joy, I just knew it was a wonderful feeling. I realized then, that I was getting telepathic messages during meditation. In one particular message, the image of Mother Mary appeared advising that I ask Wanda, a member of our group, to teach me hand positions on how to perform healings. Wanda was reluctant to do this at first but eventually she agreed to teach me. One Saturday night she gave instructions about hands-on healing to the group. Another member of the group brought a bell because he said he was instructed to do so by a higher being, he said he had noticed one in a shop earlier and felt an urge to purchase it. He ignored it, got in his car and drove about ten miles before he finally gave in and returned to buy it. He received a message indicating that it would be needed to initiate us students into the healing practices. When we were ready to begin, he hit the bell. I felt like someone had pushed a red hot poker through the palms of my hands they became so hot. Next, Wanda instructed us on hand positions, giving us a broad overview of the technique. She then asked for a volunteer to get on the table and Peggy volunteered. Wanda invited us to place our hands on Peggy and when I did, I started to see all these pictures in my head. I asked Peggy if she had a dog and a budgie and I described them in detail. To my amazement she asked me how I knew all that as I told her, "I am looking at them, right now!" When I realized that the images were real, I flipped out a bit and so I backed away from the healing work for a while. As I left that evening, the gentleman who had brought the bell offered it to me. He felt I should have it and I still use it to this day. About this same time I found out our little group in Dallas was associated with the Sancta Sophia Seminary and Light of Christ Community Church at Sparrow Hawk Village which is just outside of Tahlequah, Oklahoma, the home of the Cherokees. They were a nondenominational inter-faith group. I found out they were holding their annual conference in a few weeks so I decided to go. Joe had a house there and offered me a bed so I was set. A little while after I arrived, I wandered into the church and notice that on the inside of the door there was a sign asking for volunteers to work in the healing-room located there. I was now over my initial fright about it and was ready to learn more about healing so I signed up. I walked into the room at the appointed time to find six massage tables set up. Gloria was the instructor and as I entered the room she pointed to one of the tables and said, "Finbarr that is your table and your subject." "Gloria I can't do this. I have never worked on anyone before!" "That's ok," she said. "You can work with me. You stand on the opposite side of the table from me and just mirror, on your side of the body, everything I do with the subject." I did exactly that.

The next evening I showed up again at the appointed time. When I walked in Gloria pointed to a table, saying, "That is your table. Here comes the lady you are to work on." The woman introduced herself as Margaret and as she got on the table, she proceeded to inform me, "I am so glad it's you who will be working on me because in meditation this morning I got that if you would acknowledge me, I would be healed." Talk about pressure! I wanted to run. Instead, I invoked a healing prayer: Oh Holy Mary, Mother of God I Need Your Help and I need it NOW! And with that, an amazing white light appeared and enveloped me. My hands felt like they were on fire and I was aware of the heat spreading through my body as I focused on Margaret's form. I was astounded by this experience. Every time I opened my eyes there was this white light surrounding me. My hands were smoothly networking her body as if I had been doing this all my life. I was continuously being guided where to go next and what to ask her. Finally Gloria came over and whispered, "Finbarr, bring the session to a close as we need to go to dinner." I did so and realized I had been working on Margaret for well over an hour! As Margaret got off the table, she thanked me. She told me it was the most amazing experience she ever had, which startled me even more. I left the room and washed my hands, not saying a word to anyone about my experience. After a while, I got more comfortable with the energy as some version of that continued to happen every time I did a healing. Sometimes Jesus would appear in my mind's eye and when that happened, I knew the healing would be around forgiveness. Sometimes it would be a native shaman who would come in, and that would indicate I needed to tap into their old ways. Always, Mother Mary was there and Master St Germain who joined her in 1992 and stayed. Sometimes I would squint, softening my eyes as to better see the presence I felt, and would see it as a body of light. Sometimes I was the body of light and sometimes not. I intuitively knew where my hands had to go and how to network the body. Many times I felt as if my consciousness went somewhere else while the healing took place and I would return to awareness to find out the healing was finished. During these sessions, Mother Mary would sometimes give me a question to ask the person. Even though the question made no sense to me, it would make sense to the person receiving the healing. A huge vortex of healing opened for me, creating a profound experience for the person on the table, bringing them deep healing and a new awareness.

During the annual conference at Sparrow Hawk in 1992, I met an amazing number of people, two of whom I am honoured to call close friends to this day: Elizabeth St Angelo and Barbara Everett. Barbara once did a reading for me in which she informed me that I would run sacred sites tours to Ireland and other countries throughout the world. I asked her, "What are sacred sites? What kind of tours?" She said, "You know, you will take people to Holy Wells and places like Tara." I looked at her thinking, she is crazy. Who would pay money to go look at holy wells in Ireland? I put it out of my mind. The year was 1992 and the month was November. As for Elizabeth, she would provide me with profound assistance at a time in my life when I dearly needed it. My life was filled with reading, meditation and learning and many times I would attend some type of service at Nancy's house. On one such morning, as things came to a close, she asked for volunteers to take over some of the services a few times a month, as she was studying for the bar examination. As I drove home that afternoon Mother Mary appeared in the back seat of the car and spoke to me again. "You will lead the Aquarian Rosary on the fifteenth of August," she said. "What, me?" "Yes, you." "I'll tell you what, Mother," I respond, "I'll make you a deal. If the fifteenth of August is a Sunday I will lead the rosary. She promptly left. I wonder if I have offended her, I thought to myself. When I got home, I checked the calendar and found the fifteenth of August was a Sunday. This was significant because it was her feast day and I knew then that she was going to be a constant in my life. I had been attending services every Sunday at Golden Quest, a centre created by Joe and Nancy. On that Sunday, August 15th, I offered the Aquarian Rosary and a message from Mother Mary. This was so well received that I continued to do so once a month until I moved. I would meditate on it the Saturday night before and Mother Mary always gave me a message for the group for the next day. I would type it out and give it to the participants. Nancy and Joe were connected to Master Hilarion, an ascended master and so on other Sundays, they would give messages from him.

Eventually I moved to Sparrow Hawk full time which came about when Carol Parrish, the founder of Sparrow Hawk and the Dean of the Seminary, approached me one day and asked if I had had any experience in running a company. When she realized I had, she mentioned that the position of Chief Executive Officer had come open. She asked me if I would be interested, so I met with her and her husband Charles. He had a lot of questions and I could tell he wasn't sold on me. As I drove home that night, Mother Mary again appeared in the back seat and provided me with the answers, I relayed them to Carol and I was offered the position shortly thereafter. I became involved in pretty much every aspect of the business branch of the community where my role was mainly administrative. As part of that, once a month, I would meet with a representative from the fire department, the water department, the community association and the Home Owners Group. I would meet with them separately on Wednesdays; one week with one, one week with another as I was the representative for the church. The Home Owners Group had to give approval before any new buildings could be constructed or before any new byelaws could be introduced. They had full control of that aspect of our community life and were very suspicious of anything the church proposed. So whenever something was needed the core group, the four representatives and I, would have a private meeting in the library in off-hours. We would plan strategies to cut through the red tape and the drama which we knew would inevitably come up when new proposals were made to the Home Owners

Group. We would quietly discuss new projects, old problems and whatever else turned up that would be brought up at the next Home Owners meetings. These private meetings were usually held on the Sunday before the meeting of Home Owners Group or the Architectural Committee, as they were called. In this way we kept the wheels of progress moving forward smoothly and made it appear as if the Church was not involved. I also oversaw the gift shop, the book shop and the publishing house. The Village offered one spiritual journey a year. As the tour guide, Carol would decide which country and which sites we would be visiting and then she would turn it over to me to make it happen. This was very time consuming. I had to ferret out sources that could provide transportation from site to site, find hotels which would be comfortable, while still affordable and find out which days sites were open and their hours of operation. Along with this I had to cost out the tour as well. I worked with a travel agent but there was a lot of back and forth work involved. At the same time I was enrolled in a four-year ministerial program which meant I also attended classes during the week. The courses were intense and the work load stringent. As part of that I had an advisor who was there to mentor me and answer any questions as they came up, whether in my spiritual life or in my administrative one. She would decide which books I needed to read and in what order. I had to hand in book reports on them and I also had to write a report for the meditation committee every month. Submitting reports of my meditations to the committee was a way they could measure my progress and help me if I was having any problems with my meditation. Along with that, once or twice a week, every week,

I did healings or facilitated meditations, prayers and invocations in the evenings at Sparrow Hawk. Usually once a month I offered workshops elsewhere on Divine Feminine Emotional Healing. In 1993 Mother Mary told me that now that I knew about the positions of the hands for facilitating healing which I learned from the first training sessions with Wanda and the further training I'd received at Sparrow Hawk, she was going to teach me the networking of memory cells of the body. I had no idea what a memory cell was. Mother Mary showed me an inner picture of a grapefruit and went on to show me that even though the grapefruit was segmented, that the grapefruit as a whole with no blemishes on it represented the perfect body and that the segments represented a memory cell. Then she proceeded to turn a segment and a half of the grapefruit black. The black she said, represented disease in the body and in the memory cells. She then explained that if we were to listen to our bodies, we could heal ourselves of anything. She went on to tell me that what was held in the memory cells located in different parts of the body, meant different things. For instance, the memory cells in the left shoulder held onto blame and the right shoulder held onto a false sense of responsibility. Discomfort and pain in the memory cells of the elbows represented the need to go in a new direction. She continued on with other parts of the body, explaining to me what the memory cells of that particular body part holding a pain or issue indicated. As I began using the processes and wisdom Mother Mary had shared with me, a number of things started happening. I began, in certain instances, being guided to facilitate Soul-to-Soul conversations between husbands and wives or between parents and their children or between a person and someone who was already in Spirit. I was instructed how to work with symbols to get to the root of pain and shown how trauma could be released and healed from all the different levels of the body: physical, emotional, mental and spiritual. When doing sessions with clients, Mother Mary would always come in and refine things for me such as sharing that a pain deep in the shoulder closer to the spine, signified intense blame in which intense forgiveness, for self, was needed. Besides Mother Mary, other Masters and entities would show up in my sessions. I began to understand that when Quan Yin (a Buddhist deity known as the goddess of mercy and compassion) showed up, the session was going to be about love and compassion. When Jesus showed up, forgiveness was needed. Others showed up in the sessions as well but sometimes it was an image of a person who the issue was with, which was being cleared; other times it was Light Beings or Shamans coming in to assist whom I was not familiar with. What, or whoever it was, it was always however, exactly what the client needed and profound and sometimes complete healings occurred. There were even some people who came for Divine Feminine Emotional Healing sessions in the hopes of solving an issue, who had such a profound shift that they ended up having no recollection of the initial problem, afterwards.

On Tuesday mornings I would facilitate a Mother Mary Healing circle and on Tuesday nights I started doing the Aquarian Rosary and would channel messages. I would always know when a message would be coming through because I felt a tight band across my forehead just before receiving it. One year I attended a ten-week class on the Qabalah, an ancient Jewish mysticism, an esoteric method, discipline, and school of thought in Jewish mysticism. A couple of times a month I took different seminary classes if any popped up which I was interested in or that my adviser said I needed to take. Finally, in November of 1997, I became an ordained minister of the church. I felt that I had found my true home, a good community, a still place. Not only that, I found myself being guided by a love, a light and divine initiations more powerful and all-encompassing than I could ever have imagined possible. My time at Sparrow Hawk allowed me to grow spiritually and in so doing it allowed me to heal and to grow in an energetically charged and safe environment. I loved my job, even though sometimes during the very busy summer and fall semester I worked seven days a week, with maybe only Sunday afternoon off. I loved all the students who came there for classes from all over the world and the loving kindness of the people living there that I dealt with on a daily basis, the governors of the seminary and the trustees of the church, the managers and staff. I learned to dance around the community challenges at Sparrow Hawk in dealing with all the different factions within the community. I worked at it until such time as I could find a resolution that in the main satisfied all the parties. I was the churches representative and I dealt with all the negotiations and it was my job to see that everything ran smoothly. We always had projects on the go, from working to attract new students, creating class and retreat schedules for the coming year, selecting teachers for the various classes, the annual conference each November (a very important time with very interesting guest speakers), publishing books, developing more home sites for sale and updating bylaws etc. One could say there was never a dull moment as each day was packed full working on fund raising which was an important aspect of life along with the needs of the church, seminary, wellness centre, bookstore, publishing company and 440 acres all demanding attention. I became known as the peacemaker and it was there at Sparrow Hawk that a one legged crow showed me and taught me that I could no longer do the dance, that the time had come for me to open my heart and voice and to fully express what I stood for. This experience with the crow completely changed my life, the crow would turn up to greet me in the morning on the days I was going to face some challenges to remind me to let go of the dance and speak from my heart with love and to allow all to be in divine order. This was one of the most valuable teachings I learned at Sparrow Hawk it asked me to walk the pathway of the heart and this pathway has served me well ever since. Winter passed and spring of 1998 was just around the corner. More and more I started to feel my time at Sparrow Hawk Village was coming to an end. The energy of the place was starting to change and I was becoming a little disillusioned. There were a few people who were vying for my position, who thought they could do things better than I could. Conflicts were occurring more often than I liked. I was ready to leave and start up my own healing practice. I was just waiting for the opportune moment.

12

THE PAST RETURNS—
MY VISION QUEST

ne day, the 13th of March of 1998, the phone rang. I answered. I had initially ended up relocating to Oklahoma in 1994 after having to choose between a lucrative job offer in Dallas, Texas and taking on the position of Chief Executive at Sparrow Hawk in Tahlequah, Oklahoma. I chose the Sparrow Hawk offer. "Hello, Finbarr? Can you come to my office? There are some people here who would like to meet you." It was my boss, Carol. I picked up my jacket and headed out the door, just like I had a hundred times before. I wondered who wanted to see me. I passed through the bookstore towards her office and waved at the manager, Debra, as I went by. I tapped on my boss's door and heard her familiar voice telling me to come in but the moment I entered I knew that something was terribly wrong. Carol was seated behind her desk, her face ashen and sombre. There were two men seated in the chairs in front of her desk, both in their early forties, one dressed in a dark suit, crisp white shirt and a dark tie while the other wore jeans and a jacket. They both stood up immediately. I noticed one was taller than the other. "F.B.I.," one announced as he flashed his badge. The shorter man stepped forward and told me his name and that he was a detective from Tahlequah, Oklahoma. As soon as I heard 'F.B.I.' I staggered. I knew it must have had something to do with International Investments but that belonged to a life-time ago and I had been so sure it was all over and done with. I missed the next few words that were said, but was immediately pulled to the present when I heard, "...and arrest you on an extradition warrant. The Home Office in London has issued the order for your extradition to Northern Ireland. This order relates to events in 1984 concerning a company called International Investments, Ltd." I felt my throat tighten. "Do you know the company I am referring to Mr Ross?" I was frozen and couldn't speak. "Sir, I will ask you once again. Do you know the company to which I am referring?" My body started to give way. I grabbed the back of one of the chairs. I sank into it as Carol gave me a glass of water. My hands were shaking so badly that water was splashing about. "Mr Ross, are you okay?" I looked at the man. "No," I managed to croak. "No, I'm not…" I thought this cannot be real! This cannot be happening! I searched Carol's face looking for something; I didn't know what, looking to see how she was reacting to all of this. Her face was blank. I heard the agent's voice. He was still asking questions, one after another. I was still trying to process why they were there. I had no idea what they could possibly want with me. The business with International Investments was over years ago. I must have spoken that last thought a loud because I heard the agent respond, "Apparently not Mr Ross, who have you ticked off? The only way this could be happening is through political manoeuvring. Somebody high up is certainly after you, who you've apparently upset." I looked back at him and thought, He's not an unkind man. He's just doing his job. He put his hands on his hips and looked down at me. "I am placing you under arrest. My handcuffs are in the car so you must come quietly." The detective from Tahlequah flashed his cuffs. I saw the glint of silver. "Use mine," he offered. The F.B.I. man responded in a quiet voice, "That's okay. We'll do it in the car. Let's spare Mr Ross the embarrassment of walking through the bookstore in cuffs."

I stared at him. I was a fifty-three-year-old man, but I felt like a terrified child. "Mr Ross," he said in a low voice, "will you walk quietly to the car with me?" "Yes," I responded. I stood up and turned to Carol. "I'm so sorry," I said. "I really believed all this was resolved years ago." She just stared at me her face hard as stone. She said nothing. The agent opened the front passenger side door and I slid in. He pulled out the handcuffs from under the seat and snapped them onto my wrists. The cold metal pressed painfully into my bones. He placed a metal chain around my back and pulled it around my waist. "Do you have to do this?" I asked. "It's regulation," he responded. I began to shake and sweat. As I watched in disbelief, he produced a pair of ankle shackles. "What are you doing?" I asked in shock! He heard the panic in my voice and in response said, "I'll leave them here." I heard the chains clang as they dropped to the floor in a pile. I sank into my seat, grateful for this small kindness. I watched as the detective climbed into the back-seat of the car and the agent squeezed behind the wheel. I heard the car doors slam and the engine turn. I felt the car speed along the highway towards Tahlequah. I heard the two men carrying on a perfectly normal conversation. They were just two ordinary men driving down the highway on a chilly spring day and for them, I wasn't there and I didn't exist. I stared off into space until the car pulled up in front of the Tahlequah Police Station. The detective got out of the car and the agent and I continued down the highway. I kept hoping I was dreaming and would wake up and laugh at the absurdity of the dream. "Where are you taking me?" I finally asked. "Muskogee Detention Facility," he informed me. "What will happen to me there?" "You'll meet with the federal prosecutor. He'll give you a copy of the extradition request and then you'll appear before the judge. After that you'll probably be released," he explained. "How long will all this take?" I inquired. "My guess is you'll be home by tonight—tomorrow morning at the latest." I thought, Ok, I can do this. I will be home by tonight, tomorrow at the latest. We hit a bump on the road and I was jolted back to reality. I felt desperately thirsty because of the shock of it all. I asked if I could have something to drink. "Sure!" he said. We pulled into a gas station. The agent locked the doors as he got out. You need not have bothered, I thought. Even with the engine running I couldn't have gotten away. He returned in a moment with a bottle of soda pop. I thanked him and he replied, "Sure!" He let out a low whistle as he started the engine. He pushed his dark sunglasses tight against the bridge of his nose. "Damn!" he mumbled. "You really must have upset somebody!" I think he knew more than he was letting on. Eventually we pulled off the road and rolled through a courtyard to the jail. Iron gates parted like the Red Sea and shut behind us. I felt fear surge through my body. There was a gate behind us and one in front, to the side was a door. The agent then stopped the car and got out. I watched as he pulled out his gun and put it in a secure lock-box just outside a door, then he walked around and opened my door as if he were a parking valet.

I twisted myself and felt my legs wobble as I got out of the car. He removed the chain from my waist and took off the handcuffs. He nudged me through the door into the building and forward into a dark hallway with a cement floor. I saw a long counter at the end of it, similar to that of a bank. The counter was partitioned into smaller stalls, each manned by an officer. I heard cursing and screaming. I turned to my right, towards the noise, and could see men crammed into holding cells. One of them was kicking the bars repeatedly and nobody seemed to care. The agent took my arm and led me up to one of the cubicles. "George Ross," he informed the officer. "Wilson (the local prosecutor) drop off his package?" "No," grunted the officer, without looking up. He was not interested in conversation. My capturer pulled me along in the direction of a cell where inside it was a man with his own problems, staring at me blankly. "Get in the cell!" ordered the agent. I complied and the door locked behind me. "Good luck!" he said as he walked away. I wondered why he always kept wishing me well. I didn't want him to leave. He was a kind man, a reasonable one, and appeared sympathetic to me and I had been hoping he could help me out of this in some way, but I knew he had his orders as I watched him walk away.

13

MUSKOGEE

hours passed as I watched people scurrying about outside my cell. When they took the other man out, they ignored me completely. I was persona non grata. I heard the guards talking and laughing with one another. I kept hearing the slamming of steel doors and the incessant echo of people yelling and cursing. It seemed pointless to me because no one was listening. Later, a tall, full-figured female officer approached me. She unlocked my door and ordered me to follow her. I did so, keeping my head down as she led me to the reception counter. She then proceeded to process me. "Name?" she asked. "Ross. George Finbarr Ross." "Address?" "Sparrow Hawk Village." "Exact address?" "110 Love Lane, Tahlequah, Oklahoma." "Medications?" "None" "Occupation?" "I'm a minister." "What kind of minister?" "Interfaith. I do spiritual work." She looked up at me. She pointed to a little room next to my cell. "Go in there and take off all your clothes. "Why do I have to take off my clothes?" "So you can be processed, Reverend," she answered. "But I was told I would be going home tonight." She asked, "Who told you that?" "The agent from the F.B.I. told me." "He lied," she said. "Now go in there and take off all your clothes." I went into the small room, about eight feet by ten feet. A small rectangular steel table was up against the back wall. The table was cemented to the floor by two steel columns. An orange plastic chair sat forlornly in one corner. I took off my jacket and then my shirt. I took off my shoes and socks, followed next by my pants. I folded them neatly and placed them on the table. I was now left in my boxers and tee shirt. Outside the room I heard the female officer talking to someone saying, "Do you know what the F.B.I. told that one? He told him he would be going home tonight!" I heard someone laughing. It made me feel more exposed than I ever thought I could be. All of a sudden I heard, "Take it all off!" I turned and saw a muscular male officer looking at me. "I said, take it all off. Now! Turn around, bend down and spread your legs." As I bent over and spread my legs, I heard the sound of latex snapping. I felt the officer's latex encased hands as his fingers violated me. I yelped in pain as I nearly lost my balance and fell forward. I winced as he pulled and squeezed each of my testicles. This is one of the most humiliating experiences of my life. "Stand up!" he said when he finished. He handed me a one-piece off-white cotton boiler suit with short T-sleeves. "Put your shorts and tee shirt back on and get into the suit!" I did as he said. I watched as he stuffed my clothing into a plastic bag. He picked up my wallet. "We'll put this in a safe place," he informed me, and then gestured for me to follow him. I followed him as he silently led me out of the room and down another cement hallway. Next,

I was fingerprinted. I watched my fingers as they rolled on the pad, saturated with dark ink. I continued watching as they were again rolled onto a white card. I saw the ink transfer my prints onto the card. I realized I was being reduced to a name and a set of fingerprints. I was returned to my cell where I waited, and waited, then waited some more. Finally, I heard my name called, a different officer opened my cell. Once more I was asked to follow someone down a hallway. This time the officer led me to a Dutch door, its upper half was open. From behind the door another officer handed me a mattress pad, about two inches thick that hung down to my toes; I folded it over my arm. The officer who was accompanying me piled on a towel, a sheet, toothpaste, a toothbrush and a comb and then I followed him down another hallway to a door. I watched as he pressed an intercom. "Ross being admitted," he said. The door slid open as he guided me through it, then it closed behind me. I followed him through an endless series of doors that opened and closed. As the doors closed behind me, I thought, there is no way out! We slowly continued on, through more hallways that twisted and turned. At one point we came around a corner and I saw a group of men in similar clothing to mine. They were scruffy and unshaven, sitting on the cement floor surrounded with litter. On the wall in front of them a television was blaring, but their attention was on me, not on the television. Heavy odours permeated the room, which was dank and musty. Finally, I arrived at my new living quarters where I looked at my small cell. It was about the same size as the cell I had been in earlier. There was a stainless-steel toilet without a seat and a tiny metal basin which stood on the left. Above the basin I saw a little piece of polished stainless steel. I gathered this was going to be my mirror. A steel shelf protruded about fifteen inches away from the left wall: that is a table, I thought. On either side of it there were circular steel seats and a small barred window was carved into the opposite wall. In the middle of all this was a small lean, black man. "I ain't gonna share my cell with no fucking white dude!" This was what my cellmate said as the officer motioned for me to enter. "You got the top bunk," said the officer. I stood there for a moment. My cellmate looked at me and I looked right back. Then he dropped back onto his bunk and laid down, facing the wall, his back turned to me. I walked to the window and looked out. I saw row upon row of neatly parked cars. It looked like an ordinary parking lot, full of ordinary cars, on an ordinary day. It was only yards away from me but it might as well have been miles. I picked up my toothbrush, toothpaste, comb and towel and placed them on the metal sill. I leaned on the basin to steady myself, thinking that I would be sick. I felt my stomach roll as bile rose up in my throat; I swallowed it back down. If I wanted to survive it was crucial that I didn't appear weak. I carefully laid my mattress on the top bunk as I tried not to breathe or make a sound. I was afraid of the man lying on the bottom bunk. I thought about trying to climb up to the top one, but was afraid if I did, I would fall and disturb my cellmate. I couldn't lift my own weight the few inches it would take. I retreated to the furthest corner of the cell and sat down. I felt the cold cement against my back as I grabbed my knees and pulled them close to my chest. I just sat there like that for a long, long time and stared up at the fluorescent light on the ceiling. I pulled my blanket around me as I ached in every cell and bone in my body; I ached in ways I had never known before.

14

RANDY, CHIEF AND BONES

fter a while a man entered my cell. He was about forty, tall and athletic, fair-haired and fair-skinned. "Hey!" he said. "Hey!" I responded. "I'm Randy" "Finbarr." He stood there staring at me. After a while he asked, "What you in for?" "A warrant of extradition." "No kidding! To where?" "Northern Ireland." "Ouch! What for?" "Something to do with an investment company." "Investment Company." "Yes." I wanted him to go away. "You want a coffee or something?" he asked. "No," I answered. He stared at me some more. "Well, if you change your mind, let me know. If you need anything, let me know. Freaking Northern Ireland? That's some messed-up stuff!" As he left, another man peered into the cell and stepped gingerly inside. He was tall, older, maybe sixty, with broad shoulders and a massive chest. His skin was dark and a thick mass of salt and pepper hair covered his head. "I'm Chief," he said. This must be the welcoming committee, I thought. Next there will be tea and crumpets. "Hear you're a minister," he said. "Yes." "Where you preach at?" "Sparrow Hawk Village. I don't really preach." "Why do you talk funny?" "I'm Irish." He stepped nearer to me and lowered his voice to a whisper. "Wanna know how it works here?" he asked. My head automatically nodded yes. "Lockdown at midnight—they lock you in your cell—you can't get out. They wake you at six and you get breakfast. Lunch and supper come pretty much whenever they feel like it. You line up at the chow line to get your tray. You can eat in your cell or in the day-room. Thursdays you can order stuff from the commissary—coffee, soup, cocoa, candy, you know stuff like that. Tuesdays they deliver it to you." "Is it free?" I asked. "Heck, no! Nothing's free, preacher! You get your people on the outside to open an account for you. They put money in your account so you can order your stuff from the commissary." "Is it always this cold in here?" I asked. "Yeah. You get used to it. You want something hot to drink?" "They took my wallet. I don't have any money." "Come on," he says. "You can owe me." I followed Chief out of the cell, across the day-room, up a flight of stairs to a mezzanine full of more cells. I followed him to his cell and watched him pull a bag out from under the lower bunk. "You want cocoa or coffee?" he asked. "Cocoa," I said. He handed me a couple of packets of cocoa mix as I stood there stupidly. I didn't know what to do next. "I don't have a cup," I told him. "Nobody has cups," he responded. "Ain't allowed to have our own cups. You gotta save the cups from the soup and use them." He handed me a used Styrofoam container. He pulled out a pack of coffee from his bag. "Come on," he said. I followed him back out of the cell, down the stairs to a small table in the day-room near one of the slider doors. I watched carefully as he opened his packet and poured it into his Styrofoam container. I watched him flip up the spout on the hot water pot. I watched as the water filled the cup and the steam rose up. As he sipped his coffee I did exactly as he did, I made myself a cup of cocoa in a little used container then I followed him over to one of the tables in the day-room. I sat there sipping my cocoa from my little soup cup as if it were the most normal thing in the world, I thought, I've lost my mind. Chief talked and talked, and talked some more and I listened as he told me how he had travelled to Ireland and how much he loved the land and the people. He explained that he was a Choctaw Indian. He went on to say that during the Irish famine, his ancestors had sent a hundred and fifty dollars to an Irish famine fund. He explained that ever since, every year, a few representatives from the Choctaw were invited to Ireland. He said the year of the commemoration of the famine he was invited, because, believe it or not, he was the Chief of the tribe at the time! He explained this was how he had met Mary Robinson, the President of Ireland! I thought to myself, this cannot be real. I cannot be sitting here in jail sipping cocoa with a Choctaw Indian who is telling me about how he met the President of Ireland. My mind was reeling. Suddenly Chief bolted up from the table. "Later," he said as he shuffled off to plant himself in front of the television, "and now, the nightly news," blared the television. I didn't know what to do. I was afraid to sit there alone and I was afraid to stand up. I didn't know if Chief was crazy or a liar. I didn't know what crime he had committed. I only knew I wished he had stayed there with me. I found my way back to my cell. My cell, Holy God, I thought, I have a cell? My cellmate didn't talk to me and he didn't look at me. He hates me, I thought. He wants me dead, I was sure. A guard came by and handed me a manila envelope containing my extradition papers. I tried to read them, but couldn't. I slipped them under the mattress on my bunk and climbed up. My cellmate told me, in no uncertain terms, exactly where I could put my foot for climbing up. I paid careful attention to that. I lay there on that bunk, in the cold, trying to remember what I was thinking when I had woken up that morning. I tried to remember how the hot water in my shower felt as it cascaded over me and the way the air smelled when I walked out of my house. I tried to remember, but it seemed too long ago to recall. Hours, or what felt like years later, the light above me went out. "Lock-down," blared a voice over an intercom. I heard the screech of slider doors opening, then banging shut with the sound of the metallic click of the locks. I heard the sound of the guard walking through the tank and the rattle of door handles. I saw the beam of his flashlight as he shone it to light his way. I heard the sound of his footsteps recede as he moved further and further away. Then I heard the final slider door close and that was when pandemonium erupted. Someone, somewhere, was kicking a door. The sound of it swelled as others joined in the chorus. I heard every type of obscenity shouted out, some sexual, some racial, some ethnic, some of which I had heard before and some of which I hadn't. "Shut the fuck up and go to sleep!" the intercom squawked over the din but it only served to feed the frenzy of sound. I heard metal on metal under the voices. I heard muffled cries, anguished screams and the intonation of prayers and curses. All these flowed like rivers into a great ocean of sound, which surrounded me. It swept me under and seemed to block out anything else that had ever existed for me. Hours later, I lay in my bunk watching the dawn as it spilt through the bars of the window. I heard the buzz of the cell door as it unlocked. I heard the intercom crackle: "Breakfast! Breakfast! Get up!" I lay there trying to be invisible as I watched my cellmate stumble from the lower bunk, splash water on his face, push the door open and disappear into the parade of men ambling towards the slider. I climbed down from my bunk. I felt my feet touch the icy cold of the cement floor. I felt the sting of tears behind my eyes. I blinked them away and joined the rest of the inmates shuffling toward the chow line and I waited and said nothing. When someone later handed me a tray of food, I took it, joining Chief and Randy sitting at a table. "How was your first night?" asked Chief. "I've had better," I said as I pushed the food around my tray. "You'll get used to it," said Randy. "I don't intend to be here that long," I responded. Chief and Randy both laughed at that. Others at the table laughed as well. I looked down at my tray and didn't look up until the laughter subsided. My face was flushed with anger. When I did look up, I noticed that Chief was calmly looking at me. "You don't know much," he volunteered. "I know I'm not guilty," I said. "Don't have to be guilty," he countered. "Don't have to be convicted. The only ticket for this game is the one the prosecutor writes. Prosecutor writes that ticket and it's golden. Welcome to the jungle!" I sat there listening to them squabbling and thought, I don't belong here. "I intend to do something about this," I repeated. Chief just looked at me. Very slowly and carefully he spoke to me, as if I were a child. "The only thing you'll do, preacher, is wait for them to ask you to jump. And when they do that, when they ask you to jump, the only thing you'll say is, How high?" "But my rights —" "You have no rights. You're at their mercy, preacher. You'll do what they say and when they say to do it." "What do you mean?" I asked. "Well," Chief informed me, "the first thing that happens is, you meet with your probation officer." "I don't have a probation officer, "I told him. "Sure you do," he said. "Everyone's got one. Then you need an attorney. You got an attorney, preacher?" "No." "Better get one. They'll take you up in front the judge sometime in the next forty-eight." "And you better call someone from the outside. Can't do anything without someone from the outside helping." "How? I haven't any money!" I told him. "Use the phone in the day-room," advised Chief. "Operator places the call collect. And take a shower, preacher, you smell like crap." I burned with shame because I knew it was true. "I'll loan you soap and stuff," said Randy. "Pay me back when they set you up at the commissary." I thanked him and then felt the tap of someone's hand on my shoulder. I turned my head to see a tall man in his forties. "You going to eat that?" he asked, pointing to my tray. I shook my head. "Give it to me," he said. "Anything you don't eat, give it to me." I handed him the plastic tray and he shuffled away. "Who is that?" I inquire. "Bones," said Chief. "That's Bones."

Later, I stood in front of the phone, trying to remember the numbers of people who loved me. There were only two numbers which came up, one for an eighty year-old friend who sat on the governing board of the seminary, and the other number was Julie's, my friend from the seminary, who was married to an Irishman, Matthew. I thought, I certainly can't call this poor eighty-year-old woman and tell her I've been arrested, so, I called Julie instead. I heard the phone ring. After three times I heard "Hello?" It was Julie's warm and soft voice. Then I heard the crackle of a recorded message: "Be aware that you are talking with an inmate of a correctional institution." My heart stopped. I was an inmate. I felt shame burning in my face. I wanted to hang up the phone. "Hello?" I heard again. "Hi, Julie," I said. "This is Finbarr." "Finbarr? Where are you?" "I'm in jail, Julie. I'm in jail in Muskogee." "Who are you visiting there?" she asked. "I'm not visiting anyone, Julie," I told her. "I've been arrested." "Arrested? You're joking!" "Julie, listen to me. I've been arrested and am to be extradited to Northern Ireland." "Northern Ireland? Finbarr, what are you talking about?" "It's to do with a company that went into liquidation long ago, Julie. Julie, I'm in trouble. I need help." "Oh, my God, Finbarr! This is a nightmare! Where are you exactly?" "I'm in the Muskogee Detention centre and I need an attorney, Julie. I need an attorney right away." "Okay, no problem, Finbarr. We'll work this out. This has got to be a mistake. We'll figure this out, Finbarr. I'll talk to Matthew and the others and see what we can do! Call me back as soon as you can." I came back to my cell to a greeting from my cellmate, "You don't belong in here, motherfucker! Get out before I take you out!" I didn't say a word as I was afraid of getting him angry or provoking him. Instead I climbed up into my bunk and wrapped the thin blanket around me and I pulled out the extradition papers, 'The Book of Evidence' as it was called. It was about two inches thick, filled with the depositions of Frank and others. I was only able to read a bit before I felt sick. None of it was true; it was a pack of lies and read like a cheap novel, only I was the villain who was being accused and condemned in page after page. I thought to myself, this would be funny if it weren't for the fact that I was lying on a bunk above a man who wants to kill me… That man is right about one thing, I thought, I don't belong in here. On that we both agreed. Later that morning I heard my name called over the intercom and hurried to the slider. The guard who was monitoring the tank from inside a glass tower pushed a button. The door opened and another guard brought me down the corridor to a door. He opened it and motioned for me to go in. It was a small room with nothing but a wooden table and two plastic chairs. In one of them sat Robert Johns, an accountant from Sparrow Hawk. I was so happy to see him as he was my connection to the outside world. I knew he would have news from Julie: she had trained him and they were close. He was able to find out what was going on and would bring me whatever I needed. I was embarrassed by my prison garb but got over that quickly. He handed me a package containing underwear, socks and sneakers as well as the Aquarian Rosary Book that my boss, Carol, had sent along. Then he told me about the furore my arrest had caused at the Village, the gossip that was spreading, and the theories that were forming. I watched his lips moving but my mind drifted. It was painful sitting there listening to my friend talk about a world that no longer existed for me. Lunchtime came around. I was handed French fries and sausages but I had no stomach for it. Noticing this, Bones appeared, his lips chapped and raw from licking them too much. He took the food and stuffed it into his mouth with his fingers. In the background I became aware of swearing and cursing, voices escalating in anger. The air became thick with tension so I just kept my head down trying not to make eye contact with anyone. I remembered sitting at my father's table feeling like this, waiting for something to explode. I remembered Aunt Theresa telling me how there never was a bad person, only a person who hadn't met his good. That was what I was focusing on while I stared down at the metal table as I heard the dull thud of fists on skin and trays hurled through the air. There never was a bad person, Finbarr. I was trying to stay invisible when I heard, "Lock-down! Lock-down!" I felt myself being carried along a river, being pushed and shoved and moved towards the slider. Everyone headed towards their cells. Once I was back in my room, I peered through the small window and watched as four guards barrelled into the day-room. I heard muffled voices as I saw the guards surround two inmates. I watched as one dropped to the floor, and heard his screams as he clawed at his face. Handcuffs glinted as the guards dragged both of them into the showers. I still heard the screams above the rush of the water hitting the cement floor. Eventually the screams faded away as the guards shoved them out of the showers, down the corridor and through the slider. It was over. There was only silence. "Where are they taking them?" I wondered aloud. "Cooling off cells. Downstairs," I heard and realized it was my cellmate. It was the first time he had spoken to me other than to curse or threaten. I went very still and didn't turn around. I just stood there peering out the small window, then cautiously, I asked, "Why did they throw them in the showers?" "Gets the pepper spray off them." Later I found out that whenever a prisoner hit a guard, they were pepper-sprayed in the face so they could be controlled. Then the only way to get the pepper-spray off was to throw them in the shower. But at that point I didn't know all the details. I didn't say anything else for a long time. I was just grateful my cellmate had spoken to me in a normal voice and not in rage so I was scared to say anything and lose my quiet moment. After a while, I finally said, "Thanks very much." He didn't respond so I continued to stare out of the small window, feeling the emptiness of the tank. I just stared. Later I found myself sitting in a plastic chair at the table in the visiting-room. A strange man with a long ponytail introduced himself as John, informing me, he was my probation officer. I was thoroughly confused. "Why are you here?" I asked. "Why do I need a probation officer?" He explained that he needed information in order to complete a report for the courts. He started to ask me questions. "What is your full name?" "George Finbarr Ross." "How much money do you have?" "Why do you need to know that?" I questioned. "Do you own your own home?" "Why is that relevant?" "How much do you make?" "Why do you have to know that?" "Assets?" Finally, I just said, "I don't want to answer your questions, I want to speak with an attorney." "That's fine. I understand. Is this your first arrest?" "It is, and I don't want my rights violated," I said. He explained that I would have to answer the questions eventually but if I wanted to speak with my attorney first, he fully understood. He suggested I contact my attorney and that he'd be back later. A few hours later I called Julie again and as soon as I heard her voice I felt better. She told me that she was calling all my friends, who were shocked at what was happening and that they were working together to get me an attorney. I asked her to call my son in Dallas and my brothers and sisters in Ireland. She promised she would and told me not to worry that she would see me soon. I could barely speak. I managed to thank her but was afraid to say much more as I felt so close to tears. I knew I couldn't succumb because that would have been fatal in this place. At dinner I sat with Chief, Randy and Bones: they were my new friends now. I ate an apple and a piece of cake. The rest looked like worms swimming in watery ketchup so I gave it to Bones. He slurped it up quickly. "How'd it go with your P.O.?" asked Chief. "P.O.?" I responded. "Probation officer," explained Randy. I wondered how they knew I had seen a probation officer. I wondered if there was anything I had done that they didn't know about. "I didn't tell him anything," I said. "I told him I wanted to speak with an attorney first." "Good," stated Chief. "What was in your package?" queried Randy. I now knew, with certainty, there were no secrets in the tank. "Underwear." "Four pair" asked Chief? "Yes. How'd you know that?" "Only allowed four pair," answered Randy. "How do I wash them?" "Laundry gets done twice a week sometimes. Mostly once a week," explained Chief. "You mean we have to wear the same shorts two or three days in a row?" My new friends taught me how to survive. They taught me how to mark every item I owned with an indelible ink pen that I was given and how to make a visitor's list. "You can put seven names on that list. You can change that list once a month but give it to Polly." Polly was the guard in charge of the cleaning crew. She was tall and skinny with stringy brown hair. "Don't give it to any other guard but Polly" they told me. I discovered that Polly was the only one you could trust to deliver a note to a particular staff member downstairs in the administration, where the note would be read and passed around. They taught me how to watch my back always. They taught me to remember that I had no rights and to trust no one. They explained that being in jail was different than being in prison. You are placed in jail in the local city or Sheriff's department while you await trial. Once you were convicted you're sent to prison. In jail you are permanently confined to the day room and your cell, with bad food and no place to exercise. This new group of friends of mine taught me things I never thought I would have to learn or know about. One day, Jack Mike, a big man, the jail superintendent, stepped into my cell. He was wearing a dark ski jacket and corduroy pants. His face was flushed and glowing. I thought he looked like he had just stepped off the slopes somewhere. Maybe earlier, I mused, he might have been sitting in front of a big warm fire sipping brandy and smoking a cigar. I shivered in my cotton jumpsuit with its short sleeves. He seemed to be interested in my case—fascinated, in fact and he said the whole police force was as well. He talked to me as if I was some sort of celebrity with an energy and enthusiasm that I couldn't understand. He talked to me, about me, as if I was a third person. "Never had an international extradition in Muskogee before," he informed me. "Thought the statute of limitations would have run out on this sort of thing years ago," he said. "Really unbelievable stuff, all of this. Big time for Muskogee." Usually the statute of limitations ran out either in five, or ten years, depending on the offense. My alleged offense took place fourteen years before. I stood there looking at him blankly. He sounded like he was talking to me at a smart cocktail party or at a community fund-raiser. I wondered, does he not realize that the two of us are standing in a cell? He finally stopped for a moment. I said nothing. He looked uncomfortable in that silence and I thought, Let him be uncomfortable. He wasn't the type to be silent long. "So..." he uttered. I said nothing. "So... " he began again. "So you got yourself a big time lawyer yet?" "No," I told him. "Huh." I knew he was waiting for me to say something else. I didn't. He filled the silence again. "So, tell me again, what did you do up there at Sparrow Hawk?" he said. "I was in charge of the business operations for the church and the seminary," I offered. "Really? Wow! Sounds interesting!" he responded. "It was," I agreed. "Okay then," he said. He handed me the books Robert Johns had left earlier. Then he pulled out a pair of plastic rosary beads and handed them to me. These were the Aquarian Rosary beads. "Well," he commented, indicating the beads, "I guess it is okay to give you these then. But be careful with them. Make sure you use them for only what they're intended for." I had no clue what he meant at first. I only knew of one thing that rosary beads were intended for. He recognized the puzzlement on my face and elaborated, "Could be dangerous goods, if you get my drift." Now I knew what he meant. If someone wanted, they could remove the beads and use the string to strangle someone. "Understood?" he asked. "Understood." "Okay, then. Well if there isn't anything else you need, I'll let you go about your business." As he turned to leave, I quickly spoke up. "I need another blanket." "How many you got now?" he asked. "One." "Huh. Supposed to have two," he told me. "See what I can do about that." I thanked him. "Need anything else, just send me a note," he responded and then was gone. The blanket showed up the next day.

That night I couldn't sleep. I tossed and turned and wrapped myself in my thin blankets, freezing. I thought of the absurdity of my situation. How could I have been falsely accused of committing crimes which allegedly took place fourteen years ago? Nothing made sense. If it hadn't been happening to me, I never would have believed it. I thought about my son in Dallas and wondered how he would feel when someone told him what was happening. I wished I could have seen him and told him myself, but I couldn't, I couldn't even go to the bloody parking lot a few yards away. The next day I found out I had an attorney. "Be aware that you are talking with an inmate of a correctional institution" I heard once more as I was talking to Julie on the phone. I thought about how quickly I had gotten used to the sound of that, and everything else for that matter. Julie informed me she had found me an attorney from Tahlequah, Mr Bakker. She mentioned he would be meeting with me soon and that my friend Mary was on her way from Seattle to see me as well. She told me that she, Mary and all my friends loved me and were praying for me. They were going to end this nightmare, she promised. I listened to her voice on the line but my head was throbbing, as if someone was beating a drum inside it. I tried to hang on to the sound of her calm and caring voice. "Lock-down!" "Julie," I said, over the pounding of the drum, "Julie, I've got to go—it's a lock-down!" "A what?" Julie asked. "A lock-down," I repeated and hung up the phone. Rules were rules. When the lock-down was over I called her back. She told me that Robert was driving west from North Carolina and that Mary had arrived. She put her on the phone and Mary told me everything would be ok and would work itself out. "When?" I asked. "Soon," Mary responded. "Just have faith, Finbarr. Have faith." When I hung up the phone I felt like I was standing on the other side of a great divide. Across the abyss stood Julie, Mary and Robert. I wanted to believe I could cross that divide but every flame of hope seemed to have been extinguished. Outside the dirty window of my cell the sun was making the cars in the parking lot glitter like jewels. Faith lived on the other side of my window, but that was barred and I couldn't reach it. Carol Parrish finally came to visit. She was sitting across from me and trying to help. "What about meditating? Have you tried meditating?" she asked. "Finbarr, you need to remember to call on your inner guidance and all that you have learned at the seminary. These are the things that will help you meet this challenge." "I've tried everything I know," I responded. Maybe that was the truth. Maybe it wasn't. "You know that when we pray, we talk to God, and when we meditate, God talks to us," she lectured. I wanted to tell her I was trapped in a cell; a cold, freezing cell and couldn't think of anything but the cold. I couldn't explain this to her though. So I said, "I can't pray." "Well then, I'll pray for you," she informed me as she left. "I'll visit you again soon. Goodbye!" I had been praying, though. It was the only thing that kept me sane. It was just that, after a bit of time, I would drift off and come back with a jolt when the horrendous noise of the sliders would startle me awake.

15

MR GREEN AND MR BAKKER,
ATTORNEYS AT LAW

That evening I met my attorney and he brought another one with him, Mr Green who was from Muskogee. I asked Bakker what was it I had to do to get out of this place. He told me it was complex and that neither he, nor Green, had ever handled an international extradition before. They thought they would need to get an international attorney from Washington D.C. "Your case is a difficult one, full of intricacies and legal labyrinths" he explained. "Well, we're in a bit of tangle." "Sure are!" agreed Green. "How do we untangle it?" I wanted to know. "Well," Bakker said, "we've been trying to make sense of all this, and to tell you the truth it's pretty heady stuff. What was the International Investments, anyways?" I explained everything, that it was based in Gibraltar, that it invested in real estate in Ireland and the United States. It invested in fine art, in the London Stock Market, and that it brokered commercial loans and second mortgages. "When was the last time you had any contact with anyone from the company?" queried Bakker. "Nineteen eighty-four," I said. "Nineteen eighty-four?" "Nineteen eighty-four," I repeated. "Well, I'll tell you this, Mr Ross, tomorrow we go to court to try to secure the time we need to prepare your case. We're going to need to get the extradition papers and give them a real good look." "You haven't read the extradition papers yet?" I asked in disbelief. "Well, no. Frankly even when we do read them, I can't see as how we're going to be able to make much sense of them, we're going to need somebody who knows this stuff. We're going to need a guy who knows this international law." That was when I realized I wasn't going anywhere anytime soon. I knew it, but still I had to ask. "Are you saying I won't be released when we go to court?" "Not this time. Be patient." As they prepared to leave, Mr Green piped up, "I have one question, Mr Ross." "What is it?" "When you say Gibraltar, do you mean, like, the Rock of Gibraltar—like in Spain?" he asked. "Yes," I said wearily, "like in Spain." It slowly began to dawn on me I was in a much bigger hole than I thought I was. Now I found that the number one trial attorney in the Muskogee area, tells me that this case is way above his head and that I would need an international attorney. It became clear to me my case was much bigger than I ever imagined in my wildest dreams. The next morning after breakfast a guard wordlessly escorted me from the tank. I had no idea where I was going or why, or what was happening. He took me downstairs in front of the room where I had initially been stripped and searched. The guard told me to go in but I didn't want to: I didn't want to be violated again. I stopped in front of the door but the guard pushed in me in and there were two men waiting there. One was tall, dark and muscular, he was wearing a well-cut dark suit, a crisp shirt and a flashy red tie. The other man was shorter and also muscular. His close-cropped hair was so pale it was almost white. His face was deeply tanned and his eyes were sky blue. "Undress," ordered the taller one. "Who are you?" I asked. "Federal Marshalls. We'll be taking you to court for arraignment. Take everything off, shorts, socks, shoes, everything." I was a non-entity to these men, just a package, so I did as they said. I stood naked in front of them, fully exposed as they looked on, completely void of expression. They both pulled on latex gloves. "Open your mouth," directed the shorter one. "Lift your tongue." I felt his fingers sweep my mouth, go under my tongue and then down the back of my throat, then he was done. "What's this?" he asked as he noticed and lifted up the Aquarian cross and the Mother Mary medal that dangled from around my neck. "You can't wear anything around your neck when you're extradited," he said. "Well then, I won't be extradited," I stated. "I won't take them off." He ignored that. "Lift your arms up," he bid me. I felt his hands run up and down my body. The dark-haired Marshall watched with a vacant expression. "Turn around, bend over, and spread your legs." As I did, I felt his fingers jabbing away at me. I saw the Aquarian cross and the medal of Mother Mary swaying gently in front of me. With unspent tears I mourned my previous life as this one was filled with dark and evil days. "Northern Ireland versus Ross," I heard, standing before the judge in my short-sleeved cotton jumpsuit, in handcuffs that were attached to a chain around my waist. They, and the iron shackles, around my ankles cut into my skin. No one addressed me directly. I could have been invisible as my attorneys rattled on. "This case is adjourned until the sixth of April, 1998," said the judge. The air went out of my lungs. I felt abject despair. I wasn't possibly getting out for at least another three weeks. When I got back, Randy and Bones were waiting for me. Randy wanted to know what happened in the court. I filled him in. Bones listened and said nothing but Randy was curious. "Which Marshals took you over?" "How should I know," I said. "Well, what did they look like?" As I described the Marshalls, Randy's head nodded up and down as he figured it out. "Superman," he informed me. "Superman?" "Yeah, we call him Superman on account of how he looks all dolled up in that fancy suit with the white shirt and his bright ties." It seemed Superman was a snappy dresser and had a wide selection of flashy ties. Randy continued, "Whenever you have a complaint about the way you are being treated in the tank you should tell Superman or one of the other marshals." "Why would they care?" I wanted to know. "It's their ass on the line," he came back with. "Ultimately they gotta answer for whatever happens to us—we're federal prisoners—that's why we're here instead of in the general population." "We're all federal prisoners?" I was shocked. "Sure," explained Randy. "Every one of us has been accused of some interstate crime —except for you and Chief. You're international and Chief's an Injun." "What's Chief in for?" I enquired. "Sexual harassment. They got me on drug-trafficking." Bones started laughing his crazy laugh. "I'm a cook," he said. "A cook?" I didn't understand. "Since when is that a federal crime?" "When you cook meth," answered Bones. "Meth?" I had no idea what he was talking about.

16

BILLY JACK

Spring came and although it was bright outside, inside the tank it stayed cold. The steel of my bunk still felt like ice when I touched it. Ours was a corner cell and the walls were stone. The guards kept the temperature as low as they could because germs had a hard time living in that environment. When it froze outside, I would shiver and my teeth would chatter. After a while the cold just settled inside my muscles, into my neck and shoulders and down into my spine, where it stayed. On one particular day, more inmates arrived than had left, which resulted in a shortage of beds. There were three more newcomers than available beds. The guards decided that the three were going to have to sleep on the floors of occupied cells. One of these, a black man, was relegated to my quarters. My cellmate was pleased to have someone with whom he could enjoy solidarity. They didn't talk to me or look at me. I was used to having one black man ignoring me, scorning me, now there were two. This continued for about ten days until one morning, a group of inmates were shipped out to the transfer centre in

Oklahoma City and the cell next to mine became empty. The guard informed me it would now be my new home. I was in seventh heaven! I didn't have to live in that hostile environment any more. I was going to have my own space! Shortly after I was moved, a new cellmate was ushered into my cell, a black man, who took one look at me and starting banging on the door. "Yo, guard!" he yelled. "Look, no offence here, but this nigger ain't bunkin' down with no cracker!" Before I had much time to react, a guard appeared. I was really surprised as usually the guards ignored us. He escorted the man out and a few minutes later returned with another man, who staggered into my space. He was white, slim and had sandy blond hair. His eyes darted about and he licked his lips repeatedly. I found out his name was Billy Jack. He mumbled something else, but whatever it was I couldn't understand what he said. I wasn't worried though. I knew he would continue to mumble and I would have ample time to fathom what he was trying to say. That was the only thing I knew for certain: I would definitely have time. Billy Jack was always first in line for chow. Every morning he leapt from his bunk and raced to be the first to grab his tray. He'd sit down and gulp whatever appeared without even seeming to swallow it. He'd down his water and in a matter of moments would leap back up and race back to the cell. Once there, he'd remove a tee-shirt from under his mattress and wrap it around his head so that it covered his eyes and ears. He'd then lie back down on his bunk and immediately fall asleep, only to wake up around two in the afternoon. Then he'd plant himself in front of the television in the day-room and would just sit there without talking, staring intently at the Jerry Springer Show or whatever else was on.

When that was over, he'd return to the cell and sleep until dinner. Then he'd sleep again till about eight in the evening, when he'd rise like a vampire and reappear in the day-room to play cards or to watch television until lock-down. I watched him follow this routine day after day. Finally one night I asked him why he slept so much. "Screwing the man," he said. "What do you mean?" He repeated it and I still didn't get it. "The man is the government and I'm screwing the freaking man!" "I don't understand," I said. "Look, when I'm sleeping, they ain't got me, right? They ain't got me so long as I'm sleeping. I sleep three quarters of my time here, then they only got me one quarter, see? You still don't get it? I only serve one quarter of my time! It's sweet. It's sweet how I'm screwing the man." I laid there in the dark listening to Billy Jack's strategy. Good for you, Billy Jack, I thought. Good for you!

I always received much more mail than the others. I got letters and cards from friends who told me they loved me and not to lose faith, to be strong. They told me that everything would work out okay in the end. If it wasn't okay, then it wasn't the end. I loved my friends and was gratified and grateful that they were writing. I wrote back, though at times it was difficult because I couldn't really explain what it felt like being inside here as they had no point of reference. Yet I enjoyed the writing although Billy Jack complained that the scratching of my pen disturbed his sleep. I couldn't help it. He slept all the time. He thought I got too many letters. He didn't get any. He also didn't appreciate my attempts at humour. He would let me know how he felt by slamming himself against the bunk. He'd twist and turn and let out great heaving sighs.

Bones began visiting me around that time, at least twice a day. He'd sit on the toilet and ask me, "What's happening?" "Same old, same old," I'd say. Billy Jack would writhe on his bunk. "Can't you two shut up?" he'd snarl. "I'm trying to get some sleep here. I just ignored him and so did Bones. Billy Jack hated Bones. I had no idea why and I really didn't care, Bones was my friend. During one of his visits Bones said, "Did you know I used to be a martial arts champion?" "No!" I responded in surprise. "No, Bones, I didn't know that." "Yes, I was," he reiterated. "I was a real hot-shot martial arts champion. It started back in grade school and by the time I was sixteen my grandmother cleared out a space for me in the back of her furniture store. I used to give lessons. I got paid for that. I had my own business when I was sixteen." "That's impressive, Bones." "Yeah, it is," he said. "It's impressive." Then he got quiet for a bit. His eyes roamed over the cell and landed on the stack of books I had under my bunk. "Man, you have a lot of books," he remarked. "Yes." "That's impressive, too," he told me. "Any of them books got pictures?" "I think so." Bones loved his pictures, he was a visual man. I reached over and handed him one of the books with illustrations, a book about the hidden mysteries of the resurrection. "Is that like Easter?" asked Bones. "That's right, Bones, it's just like Easter." "I think the problem with most Christian folks is that they get all caught up in the misery of the crucifixion," Bones informed me. I was surprised to hear him say this and asked him what he meant. "Well," he continued, "anybody can get caught up in the misery of being crucified. Seems to me the real deal is to try to move through

108

that to the joy of the resurrection. I mean, when they went down to the tomb and all, Jesus wasn't even there. There was a big stone and somehow it got rolled away. Seems to me that's the stuff people ought to be getting caught up about." I listened to him and was surprised at the depth of his insights. The type of man he portrayed when he was around others was very different from the man who would sit on his own with me, discussing a wide variety of topics. Sometimes we would talk for two hours or more. Billy Jack did not like that, but he was afraid of Bones. "Can I borrow this?" Bones asked, holding the book. "Sure, Bones," I said. When he left, Billy Jack let out a loud snort. "Don't know why you bother with that half-wit," he said. "He's useless, absolutely useless." "Maybe not," I responded. "Maybe not." I continued praying every morning. I meditated and found that gradually my meditations went deeper and became quieter. I prayed for guidance. I missed the ease of small, every day, rituals. Before, in my previous life, shaving, doing laundry, changing towels was just easy and I did them without fuss when they needed doing. Here, I had to get used to being forced to use the same wet and damp towel for over a week and having to walk around the tank half-naked on laundry day freezing, while all my clothes, my four pair of shorts and socks and boiler suit were thrown into the vat for cleaning. I had to get used to only being able to shave every tenth day, even though I was used to doing it every day. Here, I was given a disposable razor and after I finished shaving I had to return it to the guards where they threw it into a big box with all the razors of all the other inmates. It was impossible to shave a ten-day growth with a dull disposable razor, which had been used untold times before, by

an untold number of men. I got used to eating cold and
unappetizing food. I got used to the guards conducting random
strip searches. I never got used to the injustices, though, and the
heart-breaking events that I witnessed or heard of. One poor
inmate refused to go downstairs when he was called for
sentencing. He refused because he had not been allowed to shave,
even though he was told he would be able to. He feared that his
unshaven face would make him appear less sympathetic to the
judge. The Marshalls came in and got him and he was forced to
go anyway. He returned, still unshaven, with an additional three
years added on to his original sentence. I realized that the beliefs
I had regarding the justice system were nothing but a child's
fantasy: it was crooked. I became aware of all kinds of injustices.
I realized that most cases never went to court because the
prosecutors wanted to avoid court at all costs. It was expensive
and time-consuming. There was also the possibility that
someone might be acquitted. Manipulation and extortion were
the tools of the prosecutor's trade. Conviction was all that
mattered, so court was a prosecutor's last resort. It was
unpredictable. Threats against loved ones and family members
proved to be more effective. I watched one man agree to the
prosecutor's terms because the prosecutor told him that if he
didn't, he would make sure that Child Protection Services would
remove his children from his wife's care. The poor man buckled
under the intimidation and took the plea. He agreed to serve
seven years for a crime he didn't believe he had committed. I
heard a story about another man who had been arrested with
his wife on charges of drug dealing falling prey to the same
tactic. He and his wife had been pulled over by the police who

searched the vehicle and their home where the closest thing to drugs they found was an over the- counter cough medicine. Angered by their inability to find evidence to back up their investigation, the police conducted a thorough strip-search on the man's wife. She attended the local church regularly but when the news of her arrest and strip-search reached the parishioners' ears, she was shunned. Although she was inevitably let go due to lack of evidence, her husband was held on conspiracy charges. Because the charges were federal, the burden of proof differed from that required by state jurisdiction: suspicion of conspiracy was reason enough, under federal law, to hold someone. The prosecutor told the man that if he pleaded guilty his wife wouldn't be charged with the same thing. He agreed, even though there was no evidence as he wanted to spare his wife. During this time, I learned a lot about how the system worked. The average stay in the tank was four months and most of the accused had never had a trial: they never even had the chance to have their cases heard before a jury. They plea-bargained, were sentenced, and about six weeks later they were gone. After my meeting with Bakker, who told me I need an international lawyer, I told Julie what had transpired. She got in touch with Jack Moriarty and Joe Vaughan, who between them and people they knew, pointed me in the direction of Tom Patton, an international lawyer from Washington, D.C. He agreed to take my case. Every few days I would speak to Julie and she would relay questions from my new attorney, Tom Patton. "Tom needs to know the exact date you moved from Ireland to the States," she said. "October 1983," I answered. "He needs the date you became a citizen." "January 1992." "He needs to know why the charges were dropped against Frank Murray in 1991." "I have no idea." "Do you have any objection to Tom contacting Joe Rice, the attorney in Belfast, Northern Ireland, who had offered to assist with the case?" Joe Rice was a civil rights lawyer in Northern Ireland. He had seen in the newspaper in Belfast, that I had been arrested. He felt that he could help me because he believed my civil rights were being violated. He called me at the Muskogee Detention centre but I was not allowed to receive his phone call. He left a message for me which I passed on to Jack Moriarty who contacted him. "Tell him to do anything he feels is necessary." I said.

17

TOM PATTON AND JUDGE PAYNE

hen I finally met Tom Patton, the International Law Attorney, I was surprised to find he was about sixty years old. He was tall and thin with grey hair that fell in a wave over his forehead. He wore a dark suit and white shirt. "You know we are going to court tomorrow," he stated." "I know," I replied. I had been living and waiting for this day longer than I had ever waited for anything in my life! The days since my arrest felt long and drawn out, full of drama and anxiety. I was perpetually not knowing what was going on and what would happen next. There was constant fighting among the inmates which incurred periods of lock-down, usually twice a day. I kept expecting to be imminently released from jail, so this nightmare would come to an end. "I'm going to be frank with you, Finbarr," he said. "This is a difficult case. To be truthful, I cannot comprehend why these charges and the extradition are coming up now after all this time. The statute of limitations was up nearly ten years ago. To make matters worse, you couldn't have picked a worse place to get yourself arrested." "What difference does it make where I was arrested?" I queried. "Well, the people down here are sort of a left-over from the Wild West." "What does that mean?" "They're the sort of fellows who are fond of taking the law into their own hands, if you know what I mean. Had you been arrested back east; I seriously doubt the charges would even have been given any merit at all." "That doesn't make any sense! Isn't federal law the same regardless of what state you're in?" "In theory," Patton said. "But there are other factors, other variables in the equation." This was my first inkling that things might not be, what they appeared to be. Later that day my friend Jack Moriarty came to visit. He had travelled half way across the country to see me. He was a big man with a quick smile and dancing blue eyes. I saw him through the Plexiglas divider as he picked up the phone on his side. "You do pick some unusual places to meet," he said. I smiled at that. He was able to make me smile like no one else could. "Well, I try!" "I can't believe all this crap is coming up now after all these years; but we'll deal with it, brother, we'll deal with it." I was amazed at Jack's determination, he was always ready to deal with anything. Other friends had comforted me and promised me that everything would turn out well in the end but I hadn't really believed them. There was something about the way Jack said it that gave me hope; he became my voice and kept after the lawyers constantly; he was my champion. We have been through a lot of stuff together. "Look, Finbarr," he continued, "I feel really good about Patton. He's a good man. He knows his stuff. I think the locals are totally useless, but with Patton here, I think we've got a chance." He said something else and I laughed. On the other side of the barrier I saw Jack laughing as well. His shoulders jumped up and down a little, his blue eyes sparkled. I wanted to hug him and tell him that he was the first person to make me laugh since I had been incarcerated, but I didn't want to break the moment. When the guard told him, it was time to go, we both stood and looked at each other through the thick glass. As he turned to leave, I said thank you and hoped that he could hear me through the thick glass.

The next morning after breakfast I heard my name called. I went through the slider and was escorted down the back stairs to the little 'strip and search room'. The same procedure was followed and again I was cuffed, chained and shackled. It was no longer strange to shuffle along with shackles around my ankles. I was led into the courtroom by one federal marshal ahead of me and one behind me where I was stunned by what I saw. Forty or more of my friends lined the benches of the court, all of them wearing yellow ribbons. They were all looking at me with sombre faces. I was filled with shame and felt disgraced, I burned with humiliation and lowered my head as I was led hobbling to the defence table. Mark Green sat at the far left of the table, Tom was in the centre and I was led to the right. Tom asked the marshals to remove the cuffs and shackles, but they informed him that it wasn't their call, it was the judge's call. Tom leaned his head close to mine and told me he had never seen this level of security for this type of case before. I said nothing. Judge Payne entered the court and everyone rose. "Your Honour, I would like to request that the cuffs and shackles be removed from the defendant," stated Tom. "It's up to the marshals," he responded. "It's up to you, Your Honour," one of the marshals pointed out. The judge said nothing. There was a stiff silence in the room. After an indeterminable pause Tom sat down, I did too, disappointed, still in chains. The Federal prosecutor, Mr Wilson, began to speak. He informed the court that he represented the government of the United States against the known fugitive, George Finbarr Ross, who had fled Northern Ireland to evade justice. He introduced Sara Criscitelly, the attorney for the justice department. He then continued on, stating that the government of the United Kingdom had issued a warrant for my arrest and extradition. He read a list of forty-one offences which the government had charged me with. He described how I had willingly, and with malice aforethought, conducted fraud of innocent people through International Investments, Ltd. I thought, fugitive of Northern Ireland, what? When Tom rose and spoke, his voice was calm and modulated. "Let me state for the record, Your Honour," he said, "that it is a legal impossibility for Mr Ross to be considered a fugitive since he has lived openly in the United States, first as a legal resident and later as a naturalized citizen. Furthermore, the alleged offences stem from the period of December of 1983 through March of 1984. Even if the alleged charges had any merit, which I assure you they do not, they cannot be considered within the guidelines of our treaty with the United Kingdom. Under the terms and conditions of that treaty, any and all charges, stemming from those dates must be deemed statute barred under the relevant statute of limitations." Sarah, the prosecutor from the State Department jumped to her feet. "Her Majesty the Queen cannot be limited in her powers!" she said. "Be that as it may," responded Tom, "the warrants charging Mr

Ross with false accounting do not meet dual criminality requirements—there are no homologous statutes or mandates of reciprocity in such cases." "Dual criminality is tolled," retorted Sarah Criscitelly. "The defendant is a fugitive from justice trying to escape his legal responsibilities and culpability to Her Majesty's Government." The lawyers continued like this for some time. It was like watching a tennis match during which my life was the ball being lobbed back and forth. "Your Honour," Tom said at one point, "it is impossible for Mr Ross to receive a fair trial in Northern Ireland. Mr Ross has never been a citizen of Northern Ireland and therefore of the United Kingdom. (I had lived in Great Britain for periods of time, but not long enough for establishing residency.) Mr Ross was born and lived as a citizen of the Republic of Ireland until 1983, when he became first a resident, and later a citizen, of the United States. This warrant is both specious and political in nature, Your Honour. It was not issued until fourteen years following the alleged incident. The Director of Public Prosecution in Dublin investigated this case years ago and found there to be no cause to be answered. "Mr Ross moved from Texas to Oklahoma in 1994, ten years subsequent to the collapse of International Investments. He has naturally disposed of any, and all, documentation which would be necessary to prove his innocence. Do you not find it curious, Your Honour, that this issue of Mr Ross being extradited should surface at the very moment when multi-party negotiations are being conducted to establish peace accord in Northern Ireland? Does it not seem relevant to the court that a case such as that of Mr Ross's is only now being so enthusiastically pursued when such explosive and sensitive discussions between Her Majesty's Government in the United Kingdom, Northern Ireland and the Government of Ireland are being negotiated? This is a case of an innocent man whose very life and personal liberty are being manipulated for political gains."

There was a politician in Northern Ireland, Roy Beggs, who very much disliked the people from the south, the Republic of Ireland. He would not agree to be part of the Peace Accord between the Protestants and Catholics in Northern Ireland being brokered by the United States, the United Kingdom and the Irish Government. This was to not only bring about an end to all the hostilities in Northern Ireland, but would also bring about a separate Parliament established for Northern Ireland and shared by all the people duly elected. The British Government needed Roy Beggs to sign off on the Peace Accord. He was not willing to do this unless someone was arrested for International Investments as some of his constituents had lost money in the collapse of International Investments in 1984. He was upset that Frank Murray, my former partner, who was in charge of International Investments when the collapse happened was released and not charged after his arrested in 1991. He was looking to have somebody charged from International Investments and it became very clear that I'd been targeted as that person. I now understood, to my abject dismay, that this was why it kept being said that my case was 'complicated'. The prosecutors were under extreme political pressure to find me guilty so the Peace Accord would go through on Northern Ireland's terms. It wasn't about justice at all, but was purely

political. "Northern Ireland in its entirety remains a part of the
United Kingdom," said the prosecutor. "Mr Ross has never been
a citizen of the United Kingdom," countered Tom. "Frankly, I
do not know what you two are talking about," said the judge. I
was flabbergasted by this and couldn't hide my own
incredulousness. How could this judge not know the difference
between Northern Ireland and the Republic of Ireland? I sat
there and listened to the judge and the lawyers argue about
geographic and national boundaries. Finally, he announced that
he would deliberate and render his decision on the following
Friday, Good Friday. I began to sweat and wondered if I would
ever again know freedom as I was rode back to Muskogee in
chains.

Later I found myself sitting behind the Plexiglas barrier with
my friend, Jack, once again on the other side. We were both
holding the receivers in our hands, but there was nothing to be
said. We just stared at one another until finally, Jack spoke.
"Finbarr, know that I will leave no stone unturned to get to the
truth and see you walk out of here a free man, I promise you
that. I promise you I will leave no stone unturned." There was
nothing to say, so I said nothing. I just stared through the glass
at my friend Jack, amazed at his determination and his faith.
"I'm here for you. We're going to do this. I promise you that.
We're going to do this." Back in my cell my friends gathered
around me, Chief, Randy and Bones. "What happened?" asked
Randy. "I have to wait until Friday to get a decision from the
judge," I explained. "There's no way you'll have a decision by
then," piped in Chief. "Why not?" I inquired. "That's Good
Friday," said Chief. "There's no way you can know anything on

Good Friday. You'll have to wait till after Easter." "That's not fair! He said he would let me know by Friday!" I spouted. I looked at Bones and Randy hoping they would back me up. They were silent. "Trust me," said Chief. "You won't know on Good Friday. You'll have to wait till after Easter." Meanwhile my friend, Carolyn Otto came to visit me. "There's something I've got to say to you," said Carolyn. She was talking to me through the receiver on the other side of the glass wall. "What is it Carolyn?" I asked. "I'm very disappointed in you, Finbarr. I'm very disappointed in the way you walked into that courtroom last week with your head hung down like a guilty child. You have done nothing wrong; you have nothing to be ashamed of. I do not want to see you like that again. The next time you go into court I want to see you hold your head high. I want you to look in the face of that judge and those lawyers and let them know who you are. I want you to look into the faces of all your friends and accept their love and support. You owe it to yourself and you owe it to them." I felt like someone had thrown a bucket of cold water over my head, I knew she was right. I knew I had forgotten who I was. I also had a visit about the same time from Julie's husband, Matthew Tierney, who was originally from Limerick in Ireland. "Finbarr," he said, with soulful eyes, "whatever happens you mustn't let them extradite you. There's no way they will ever give you a fair trial in the north. People disappear up there, Finbarr. They disappear up there and no one ever hears of them again." "Don't worry, Matthew, I don't think we'll ever get to that stage." "Finbarr, listen to me—you mustn't go. You mustn't let them take you. If you go, we'll never see you again." "Do not be afraid, Matthew. Do not be afraid." Finally,

Good Friday arrived and so did Carol Parrish who came to give me communion. There had been no word from the judge.

18

EASTER SERVICE AND THE BIRTH
OF THE EVENING GATHERINGS

Later in the day I asked my friends if the jail had any plans to celebrate Easter. There didn't appear to be any plans for any kind of service in the tank. "Why don't you do a service for us?" suggested Chief. "Me?" "Yes," said Randy. "You're a minister, aren't you?" "Yes," repeated Bones. "You're a minister." "Yes," I confirmed. "Yes, I am." I wrote a note to Jack Mike asking for permission to use the room known as the library for an Easter Sunday service but I didn't receive a reply, so, I held the service on Easter morning in the day-room. Twelve men attended. The altar was a steel table, the chalice a Styrofoam cup, the wine cherry Kool-Aid, and the pieces of unleavened bread, potato chips. I talked about forgiveness and the need for it. I prayed with those twelve men gathered around a steel table locked in a tank and it felt good. I realized that including me, there were thirteen of us, the number of transformation. After that service, the odd inmate would amble by my cell and ask me questions. Sometimes we would just talk in the day-room, which was filthy. The more the other men and I talked, the more I wanted to take action to change the conditions of the tank. The floors and walls were covered with gunk and grime. The day-room was littered with food droppings, paper, empty potato chip bags, candy bar wrappers, and used tissues. I asked Polly daily if something could be done. Eventually, two orderlies showed up one day with a squirt bottle filled with watered-down pink ammonia, a broom, a mop, and a toilet brush. I immediately took it upon myself to start cleaning the place up, Bones joined in and so did the Chief and other men did as well. Every day we brushed, mopped, scrubbed and swept. We used Colgate toothpaste to clean the steel wash-basin and mirror. As new inmates arrived, they were told they had to keep the tank clean. Some were eager to join the effort, but others not so much. When one of the new inmates threw a piece of garbage on the floor of the day-room one day, I asked him pick it up. "Up yours!" he said. Bones walked over and picked up the garbage, he took it to the cell of the new inmate and he threw it on the floor there. He turned back to the new inmate, who stood there dumbfounded. "If you want to live in filth, that is your right," said Bones, "but this space belongs to all of us and we have made a decision not to live in garbage. If you want to, move somewhere else." The only place to move to would have been worse so I wondered how the new inmate would react. He said nothing. The next night, however, after he finished unwrapping a candy bar, he took the wrapper and threw it into the trash can. The days that followed were different and so was I. I felt something like peace, like safety for the first time in weeks. I felt a warmth inside me that radiated throughout my body. Tom Patton visited not long after. "Payne has ruled you are eligible for extradition," he informed me. "He has ruled that you are a fugitive from Northern Ireland. Being a fugitive, the statutes are tolled (waived). I'm sorry, Finbarr." "What about the false accounting charges?" I asked. "Payne ruled that they stand. He ruled for dual criminality. "I see," I said. "Jack Moriarty and I have been speaking. We're going to go ahead and file a Writ of Habeas Corpus. (A writ, requiring an arrested person be brought before a judge or into court to secure the person's release unless lawful grounds are shown for their detention.) We should have it filed within a week. After that we have to wait until the court appoints a judge to hear the case." "What does that mean?" I asked. "That means we take it to a higher court challenging Payne's ruling." "I see," I repeated. "I am sorry, Finbarr," he said. "I am truly sorry." I returned to my cell and lay down. I slept, and when I arose, I felt only half there, like part of me was missing. The peace I had known seemed like a dream and I was filled with terror once more. I was so cold I shivered, as I went through a dark night of the soul I was filled with despair. When I came out the other side, after waking up filled with despair, I knew I had to somehow come to accept what was happening to me. I realized I was having a shift of consciousness. I was grateful for all the people helping me and I had to have forgiveness for myself. This was how I found my way back to a peaceful place. I sat quietly on the cement floor of my cell compiling lists of all of the things for which I was grateful. That helped as the friction and chaos around me continued. "I'm gonna get that weasel this time!" said Billy Jack

one day. "Which one would that be?" I asked. "Bones." "Why?"
"Because he is a no-good useless piece of crap!" he answered.
The two of us were in our cell. I watched as Billy Jack pulled
half a scissor blade from beneath his mattress, he waved it in the
air. I felt fear come up in my solar plexus but ignored it. "What
have you got there?" "None of your business," he said. "Don't
worry, it's not for you. It should be for you because you are
stupid enough to give that sorry excuse all your food." I took a
deep breath. "Now Billy Jack, you know I give you food
sometimes as well," I told him. He didn't respond. He just stared
at the blade, running one finger along its glinting edge. I realized
he was afraid of Bones and was jealous of my friendship with
him. "Come on now, Billy Jack, give me the blade." I put out my
hand he stared at it. "Get out of my way! Get out of my way or
I'll cut you!" he said menacingly. I noticed chief walking by and
called him in: he came quickly. The two of us tried to talk Billy
Jack down into giving up the blade, but he refused. Max, another
inmate, came in to help. All three of us talked to Billy Jack in
low voices, telling him that he would only make things worse
for himself. We told him we all knew how he felt and that we
wanted to lash out too. We told him we understood, but this
would only make things worse. After a time, he handed the blade
to Max and another day passed. Part of what precipitated the
incident was that once a week I would give Bones my food. Every
Wednesday I would fast, and every month around the full moon,
I would fast for five days, two days before, the day of, and for
two days after the full moon. Bones was the recipient of my
meals and this is what had set Billy Jack off.

Not too long after this there was a shakedown in the tank as the guards were hunting for tobacco. They strip-searched everyone and ransacked each cell. In a crack in my cell they found the blade. "What's the story behind this?" one of the guards asked. I wanted to lie but because I was afraid of the consequences, I didn't. I wouldn't be driven by fear any longer. So, I told him the truth and that Max was supposed to have disposed of it. He thanked me. The following morning both the shakedown and lockdown were terminated. By this time, I was reciting the Aquarian Rosary every night. I talked a lot with Bones about prayer and meditation. He was curious to know why I had begun doing both with such regularity. He noticed I had changed and was curious as to how I could seem so peaceful in the midst of the chaos. Other prisoners joined our conversations and something happened, I no longer felt separate and apart from these men. The number of people I called friends, had expanded. Although the tank was still damp and chilly with the rains of early spring, I found that I no longer felt the cold. My body was still cold, but I was not, I was back on track. I offered my place for anyone interested to just get together and talk in my cell. We would meet around 7:00 pm and share our stories with one another. I would read a Bible passage from a small book called the Daily Word, published by Unity. We would discuss it. If anyone had a bible, they would look up other relevant passages. We had three other books that we worked with a lot, 'The Dance of Anger', 'Co-Dependency No More' and 'You Can Heal Your Life' by Louise Hay. Then we would do the Aquarian Rosary and have a Universal Communion. We would wrap up around 11:00 pm. This was possible because, in the evenings, Billy Jack watched television in the day-room and my cell was available. A friend sent me a beautiful watercolour of Mother Mary. The men and I used it as a focus for our daily meditations. We used that painting as the centrepiece for the altar during our prayer services. Mother Mary was there with us. Through all of this I learned so much about the types of challenges men faced and the types of abuse, physical and emotional, they experienced. Being able to talk about all of this made a huge difference to all of us. For ten months, for the first time in the history of that prison, not a single fight broke out and Jack Mike, the jail superintendent was thrilled. He was very accommodating whenever Julie showed up with whatever we asked her to get us; he would turn a blind eye as items were passed to us. I even received a Shusta deck of cards which I used to do readings with. He was a good man and was open to anything, within limits, that would keep the jail running smoothly. One day Bones asked me to do some emotional healing work on him. He told me he was afraid he would never be able to turn his life around. He told me he was afraid of what would happen to him when he was sentenced and transferred out of this place. "The only way I know how to effect change is through forgiveness," I advised him. I told him that I had learned through my own suffering that, trauma and suffering affects us in our four bodies: the physical, the emotional, the mental, and the spiritual bodies. I continued on to say that I had come to believe that all four had to be healed. "As one suppresses feelings of fear and anger, they become trapped inside not only the physical body, but inside the emotional, mental and spiritual bodies as well. Bones, it is a painful thing to live trapped in a prison of one's own fear and

127

anger." "But it's not my fault," responded Bones. "It's not about fault or blame," I explained, "it's about energy trapped within the memory cells. The laws of universal energy are ruled by the Divine. There are physical laws like the law of gravity and there are universal laws, too." "But there are things I want, things I need." "I know. I know. There are things I thought I wanted and needed too. I am only just beginning to understand the truth of those wants and needs." "Yes? And what's that?" Bones inquired. "The truth, for me, is that there is nothing on this earth that is more important than working to manifest inner divinity. I think I knew that as a small boy. Each of us can blossom and unfold in our spiritual potential as we journey through life, walking our chosen path but I forgot that Bones, I was too busy picking up stones." "Stones?" he asked. "Stones. Exactly! That's what our ego wanted, to blame, accuse and think everyone else is at fault. Our job is to not cast the first stone, as it says in the Bible. Universal law demands that each of us transform from within. It really is an inside job. No one can truly force us to change or grow, or even to suffer, or be afraid. We cannot be forced because we have free will. But as we transform and choose to live in a spirit of generosity, in giving and receiving in accord with universal law, like the law of cause and effect—well, then we truly have undergone a change. We have been resurrected in some very tangible and powerful way." "Like on Easter," commented Bones. "Like on Easter," I said "Makes me think of that stone," he said. "You know, that big stone that they used to block the tomb? And when Mary came down in the morning it was rolled away and there was that angel standing right in front of her." I didn't say anything more, I just stared at the scars on his forehead. The scars were from pistol whippings he had received at the hands of law enforcement. There was something beautiful about them, I thought. It was the mark of humanity and the beauty of the Divine.

I thought a lot on all aspects of the Divine and I thought of Mother Mary as I waited patiently to hear from the courts. During one of my conversations with Julie, she mentioned that there was a letter-writing campaign being conducted on my behalf. Over two hundred people had begun writing letters in protest of my illegal incarceration. I was shocked because I didn't think I knew that many people. I was even more shocked to discover that Tom Colburn, a congressman from Oklahoma, was one of those who had written a letter seeking help. His letter was to the Department of Immigration asking if they had any interest in me. The answer was brief. "No," they replied, "Ross is a naturalized American citizen." Tom Patton told me he discovered, through research he conducted under the Freedom of Information Act, that my immigration file had been sent to the American Consulate in London in 1997. He told me this was a clear violation of the law. Immigration files are private and, as such, are required to remain in the United States.

Billy Flynn (William Flynn), a private investigator in Ireland, wrote a book about me and my situation called 'Gibgate'. In it, I was depicted as a polo-playing jet-setter, an international playboy, whose life consisted of women, wine, and untold fortunes. I had to laugh because this was nothing further from the truth. My friends, Mary and Robert, told me that they were going to go to Ireland to try to find their way through the labyrinth of lies that had been constructed about me. I doubted very much if there was any point to doing that. During one period of time, I was unable to contact Tom Patton in Washington D.C. by telephone. The prison administrator promised to encode the telephone system in the necessary way to allow me to reach him. However, that didn't happen. Weeks slowly passed and I was unable to return the calls Tom had made. Because of this failure, the communication necessary for the preparation of my case, never happened. One morning, after weeks of this, I yelled up to Mr Love, the guard in the tower. "Mr Love!" I yelled. "Has the phone system been properly encoded yet?" I already knew the answer but I had to start somewhere. He completely ignored me, sitting behind the thick glass of the tower. He continued to read his newspaper. I repeated, "Mr Love, has the phone system been properly encoded yet?" I continued this questioning every two minutes for the better part of an hour. Finally, he lost patience. "Keep it up Ross and I will lock you down!" he threatened, I continued. "Mr Love, has the phone system been properly encoded yet?" He ignored me, I continued. Two minutes later I repeated the question; he ignored me yet again. This continued for over another hour until finally, he had enough of me on the intercom and shouted, "Are you happy now, Ross? I've just called downstairs to have you removed from your cell and sent to the cooler." "Mr Love," I asked once more, "has the phone system been properly encoded yet?" Three guards burst through the slider and grabbed my arms. "What the heck is wrong with you, Ross?" asked one of the guards. "You gone crazy or what? Do you want to go the cooler?" "No," I answered, "but I am being denied my constitutional rights. The jail system is preventing me from speaking with my attorney. I have been patiently requesting that the phone system be properly encoded for nearly a month now." He stared at me and I stared back, not in defiance or in anger, just from a place of truth. He glared at me and shook his head. "If the phone system is not properly encoded allowing me to speak with my attorney, then I will have no alternative but to ask one of my friends to call the federal marshals and explain that my constitutional rights are being violated." On that, all three guards turned on their heels and disappeared through the slider. About twenty minutes later the senior of the three guards came back and said, "Mr Ross, the phone system has been properly encoded, you may now call your lawyer in Washington, D.C. Sorry for the delay." I thanked him for his help. He seemed to treat me with more respect after that. Things like this came up periodically and I dealt with them. One of the things I noticed, after a bit, was that these guards became friendlier after such an incident and would stop and talk to me. When I finally got to speak to Tom, I found out that my Habeas Corpus hearing had been set for the 14th of May. I was told that the presiding judge was a man named Burrage. Chief informed me that I was lucky. "Burrage is a good man, a good man and a fair judge." As the hearing drew near, I began to allow myself to think about life outside the cell. I asked Julie and Jack Moriarty to dispose of the few valuable possessions I still had. I was going to need money to pay for my defence and legal expenses. Over the years I had lost so much that I wasn't even sad to relinquish the last of my worldly possessions. When Robert and Mary returned from Ireland, they had a nice surprise for me. Billy Flynn, the author of Gibgate, informed them that he had come to realise I was completely innocent, he had all the necessary documentation to prove it and he wanted to help clear my name. He wanted to help me reclaim my reputation which he had previously helped to destroy by writing Gibgate. In return, he wanted the smallest of favours. He asked me to request a public inquiry into the liquidation of International Investments. He wanted me to submit a list of names which he had compiled to send to the Minister of Trade and Industry, the names of people he was certain were guilty, and who needed to be punished. I really wanted him to clear my name, I wanted him to tell all of Ireland that the things he wrote about me were nothing but lies. I looked at the list of names and knew, or at least thought, that some of the people listed had nothing to do with International Investments and I also knew it wouldn't have mattered to Billy Flynn. I knew what he would do to them would be exactly what he had done to me. There would be lies printed and reputations destroyed. I looked at that list and I looked at Mary and Robert. I wanted to have my reputation restored, but I ripped the list up into tiny little pieces. As I threw those tiny little pieces into the trash can I watched as they fluttered down like snowflakes on a winter's day.

19

BAIL AND EXTRADITION

I was devastated when my hearing was postponed again. It wasn't until the 20th day of May 1998 that I once again entered the courtroom in shackles. This time, however, I held my head high and looked directly into the faces of those around me, the faces of the judge, the prosecutor and the bailiff. I looked straight into the sea of my friends' faces and I smiled as Tom rose and addressed the bench. He reiterated that I could not be considered a fugitive of any kind since I had lived openly and legally in the United States for so many years. Judge Burrage listened carefully and thoughtfully, then he said he would give a decision in six weeks. Tom then asked about bail and the judge said he would be happy to hear a submission of bail once the necessary paperwork had been filed. Tom Patton returned to Washington and Mark Green was given the task of representing me at the submission of bail. We set about making the necessary arrangements. The Otto's, friends of mine from the Village, had agreed to let me stay at their home when I was out on bail and their telephone would be linked to the electronic monitoring system. The bail was going to be set at twenty-thousand dollars, two thousand, of which, had to be in cash. My friend, Toni, from California agreed to post it. Everything was in place and ready to go when I walked into the courtroom for the submission. I waited at the defence table. Mark Green and Wilson, the prosecutor, were in chambers with Judge Burrage. After about ten minutes Mark Green came out and whispered in my ear. "Finbarr, we have a little snag here," he said. "What kind of snag?" I asked. "Well, it looks like Judge Burrage can't let you out on bail for anything less than two hundred-fifty thousand dollars, with twenty-five thousand up-front in cash. They have agreed to that. Can your friends come up with that, do you think?" "Yes," I answered, not knowing if that was true or not. At that moment I would have said yes to anything and found a way to follow through. "Good. Well, then, OK!" said Mark Green. "Looks like we got ourselves a deal!" I sat there for a moment, sensing something was very wrong. "Where is Wilson (the prosecutor) now?" I asked. "I left him in chambers with the judge," he told me. "Mark, tell me you did not do that!" "Why?" "I am not going to get bail now." "Of course, you are, Finbarr. It's all set, it's a done deal." He had no idea that he had done the worst thing he could possibly have done in leaving the prosecutor alone with the judge. I instinctively knew if Wilson was in there with the Judge passing on some political message to him, it would get him his desired outcome of, no bail. When the hearing started it went very quickly. Wilson argued that since Payne had found me to be a fugitive fleeing from justice in Northern Ireland, it was highly likely that I would skip out of Oklahoma five minutes after the chains were removed from my hands and feet. Green argued that security had been dealt with, that electronic monitoring was all in place and arrangements had been made to make sure that I couldn't just disappear. Judge Burrage called a five-minute recess. I wondered why he needed a recess. Was he calling someone? When he returned he didn't look at me, he simply stated, "Bail denied." I had already come to understand that I was merely a pawn in a much bigger game. There were political overtones to my case that I had refused to see until this trial. When I returned to the tank no one was surprised to see me. I thought of how naive I had been.

Two days later, Billy Jack told me that he was going to send his television to the outside as he needed money for the commissary. It was his TV that was in the day-room, the prison hadn't supplied it so Billy Jack threatened to send his TV home if no one would buy it. "How much do you want for it?" I asked. "Sixty bucks," he informed me. I arranged with Julie to deposit sixty dollars into his account. In the meantime, I drew up a bill of sale and had him sign it. Another inmate, Michael Loper, witnessed the transaction. A few days later Billy Jack was sent to the cooler for fighting with the tower guard. I was moved up to the mezzanine level where Loper became my new cellmate. I had not made bail and hadn't been freed, but now I had a new cellmate and a television. I liked Loper, he was a tall, big-boned man in his thirties with dark eyes and long brown hair that flowed halfway down his back. He was a Native American Indian with a gentle voice and an easy grin who knew his Bible inside and out. I remembered how frightened I was, the first day I arrived, and how my first cellmate had hurled racial epitaphs at me. Loper was completely different and when I first entered the cell he volunteered to take the top bunk. I thanked him for his kindness and he flashed a smile. "Don't mention it. Age before beauty." While Billy Jack was in the cooler I changed the viewing schedule for the television. When he had owned it, he dictated what we watched. Now that I did, I worked it so all the inmates were given an opportunity to watch what they wanted and they were grateful for the change. The mood in the tank was more peaceful until Billy Jack returned. "It's my TV and I can watch anything I want; you weasel!" Someone had signed up to watch an old John Wayne movie but Billy Jack wanted to watch the Jerry Springer show. He wasn't interested in sharing anything. "Billy Jack," I reminded him, "don't you remember that you sold your TV to me? It's mine now and I've come up with a fair system that will give everyone a chance to get to see what they want. All you need to do is sign up in advance for any vacant slot." "Really?" said Billy Jack. "Really," I responded. "All I have to do is sign up for any vacant slot?" "That's it." "Well I'd like to sign up now." With that he slammed the full force of his closed fist into the side of my head and sent me reeling backwards against the cement wall. As I did so, I raised my hands to protect myself while he hit me again. Thankfully Bones appeared out of nowhere and wrapped his arms around Billy Jack and Billy Jack was screaming. Bones whispered into Billy Jack's ear, "I will not let you hit him again." Billy Jack glared at me as Bones pushed him down to the floor. Billy Jack picked himself up and trudged away towards his cell. I looked at Bones in thanks and appreciation. Not long after, Billy Jack informed me that he would give me a beating every single day, and he meant it. An hour or so later, back in my cell with Loper, who had been sleeping, he saw the bruises and swelling on my face and wanted to know what happened so I told him. He immediately marched down to have a chat with Billy Jack. When he returned, he told me not to worry about Billy Jack. "I told him that if he lays a finger on you again, he will have to answer to me," "Thank you, Loper!" I said. "No problem, Reverend," he responded with his easy grin. "Got to look out for one another in here, Reverend. We're all in this thing together—you know that whole 'I am my brother's keeper' thing. Know what I mean?" "Yes," I said. "Yes, I do." When the guard made his regular rounds a few hours later, he also asked what happened to me. I told him and asked him which duty officer was working and he mentioned Chrissy. I asked if he would tell her that Billy Jack had threatened to give me a beating every day and would she do me a favour and move him? Within fifteen minutes she arrived in the dayroom with two guards, Billy Jack was told to pack his stuff. "Why?" he asked. "Because I said so." I thanked her with my eyes and a nod. He was moved and I never saw him again. Outside the bars of my cell window I could see the weather change while inside the tank there were changes, too. The small meditation and discussion group that had started out with Bones, Chief and me had now grown substantially and now there were usually ten to twelve men sitting around. Todd, Danny, Johnny, Harold, Brice, and Loper had all joined the group, gathering in Loper's and my cell. Brice's wife sent us twelve copies of Louise Hay's book 'The Power within You'. The group started to study that book three times a week from two to four in the afternoon. The other men and I took turns sharing and listening to each other's stories. I spoke of my perceptions and illusions and how they were changing and dying away. The group also read 'The Illuminata' by Mary Ann Williamson, 'Co-Dependency No More' and 'The Dance of Anger'. The men discussed their various religious experiences with prayer and meditation. We prayed the Aquarian Rosary together, partook in Universal Communion service, and we meditated. I began a prayer list and a healing list and gradually our group began to see changes happening within themselves and in each other. We became more relaxed and helpful towards each other and moved towards a greater understanding of ourselves and of the will of God in our daily lives. Then Bones received his sentence. Before he was led away, he came to my cell to say goodbye. His greeting was the same as always. "What's happening?" "Same old, same old," I said, the same as always. We both laughed at this. "I was betrayed, you know," he told me. "Yes, I know." "They lied to me about the deal. I kept my end of the bargain and they lied. They tacked an extra two years onto my sentence for gun possession. They never said anything about that when I made the deal. I'm angry, Finbarr. I'm real angry!" "I know. What are you going to do about it?" "Only thing I can, accept it." "You've taught me a lot." "Really?" "Yes, Bones, really." "Wow. Nobody has ever said that to me before. Go figure!" As I looked at Bones, I knew he was not the same man I had first met. I thought maybe I wasn't either. "Well, I hate goodbyes and all. Good luck to you, Finbarr," he said. "Good luck to you, Bones." He walked out of the cell. A moment later he poked his head back in. "Hey, Finbarr?" "What is it Bones?" "Pray for me, will you?" "I will pray for you, Bones.

Six weeks later, Judge Barrage gave his decision on my case

stating that he agreed with the former Judge Payne's decision. Tom was furious and said he was going to appeal to the Tenth Circuit court. They also ruled that I was a fugitive. They had to give a decision as to why I was a fugitive, but when Tom asked why, they refused to answer him. He was very upset and said that in his career, the justice system had let him down three times and this was one of those times. He wanted to take this to the Supreme Court and he told me not to worry about the money, he would do it pro bono as he was that upset. I asked him how long the appeal process would take. He thought about eighteen months but he was sure we would win because my rights had been brazenly violated. I told him, thank you but, "I can't do another eighteen months in here. I'll go to Northern Ireland now." So it was that early one morning around 4:00 am in May, the intercom in my cell buzzed. "Ross, pack your stuff." I had been expecting this for about three weeks, ever since the Tenth Circuit had ruled. I had asked Julie to bring me proper clothes. Jack, the jail superintendent kept them in his office until I was sent for. Superman was one of the Marshalls who was sent to escort me and so we drove to Tulsa, Aquarian Cross and all. We then flew to St Louis, changed planes and then on to D.C. arriving at Regan National Airport with me still handcuffed, chained and shackled. I was then transferred to the Alexandria Detention Centre for three days where I was locked down and not allowed to speak with anyone except the person who brought my food nor was I allowed to take a shower in the centre for three days. Finally, on the evening of the third day, the Marshalls came and took me to a police station near Dulles Airport. I was later escorted to the airport where I was handed over to two detectives from Northern Ireland. These two detectives seemed to be harried and hurried as if they seemed to be waiting for something to happen and they were getting upset. "Where is he, where is he?" I heard a few times. Later I realized that they were waiting for the F.B.I. agent who arrested me to confirm that I was indeed the right man. That had to be done before I could be handed over to the detectives from Northern Ireland and escorted onto the plane. The F.B.I. agent confirmed that I was the person he had arrested and wished me well on my journey. It was just after 11:30 pm before we finally arrived at the plane with the male detective in front of me and the female one behind me. They sighed with relief once we were seated. The man turned to me and asked, "Am I going to have any trouble with you?" I said, "No. "He then took my hand-cuffs off. I was seated between him and the female detective. He explained to me that the rush was because they had to be on the British Airways plane before midnight otherwise the window to extradite me would close. Even though the State Department had known for three weeks it had to happen; they only informed Northern Ireland five days before the time limit would have passed. I surmised from that, that someone high up in the State Department didn't agree with what was going on and tried to make it difficult by only giving them a five-day leeway. If I hadn't been on board the plane that night by midnight, which was the fifth day, I would have had to have been released as they had not collected me within the time period allowed by the courts. Well, the detectives made it, but just barely with only moments left to spare. After a short stop in London, where they had a little difficulty getting me through immigration with no identity papers such as a passport or driver's license, I was flown to Belfast. As I was led down the stairs of the plane, I was greeted by the sight of newspaper reporters and television cameras. Their faces were hard as stone. The cameras flashed and the reporters pressed in closer to get a look at me. I was surprised as no one was supposed to know I was arriving. As the police car sped along the motorway, I looked at the Belfast hills and as we arrived at the Royal Courts of Justice in Chichester Street, I wondered if I could ever find justice in such a place. When I got out of the vehicle a man was standing there. The police officer said, "This is your solicitor," and Joe Rice introduced himself to me. Again he was the lawyer who read about my case in the papers because my arrest had been all over Northern Ireland. So, a week after I was incarcerated in Muskogee, he phoned the jail to speak to me and was told he couldn't. They did give him a fax number, though, and he did send a fax offering his services. I had given it to Jack, who contacted him after doing extensive research to find out who he was. When Jack was satisfied he was legitimate, he phoned him and asked him why he wanted to help. His response was, "Because here is a man whose civil rights have been violated." Joe was strongly involved in civil rights and criminal injustices. Satisfied with that, Jack passed the information on to Tom Patton and the two attorneys had started to talk. That had happened a year earlier, in the first week of my detention in Muskogee.

Now that I was in Northern Ireland, I was glad to have him representing me as we entered the court. It was packed with reporters and I listened as the charges were read, but it seemed there were two problems. The arresting officer who escorted me from Washington was not present and therefore they could not confirm I was the person he had taken into custody but finally, he arrived and that was taken care of. Secondly, the book of evidence didn't appear to be ready and couldn't be produced. My accusers couldn't even present one piece of evidence. Joe Rice tried to have the case dismissed right there and then on the basis of the failure on the part of the prosecution to provide the necessary evidence of the charges against me. The magistrate refused. With that, once again, I was led away in handcuffs. I was taken to Maghaberry Prison and had no idea how long I would be there. I knew of this place and had heard stories of the horror of this prison. This was the place where Republican and Loyalist prisoners once burned mattresses. The huge iron doors opened as the car motored into the first courtyard. Another huge set of doors parted and the car continued on deeper into the bowels of this place where I looked at the grey walls as I was processed. "Religion?" asked the guard who was filling in the paperwork. "Post-denominational," I said. "I am of universal consciousness." "What the heck is that?" he asked. "You could call it universal Christ consciousness or interfaith," I answered. "I've no idea what you're talking about," he responded. "How about if I just put down 'Other'?" Perfect. Later, this designation would allow me to attend services of all the denominations where I was able to make connections with the various ministers and priests.

As I passed the cells on the way to mine, I noticed each one had a little card posted over it, stating the prisoner's name and number, the charges against him, his status, i.e. 'Awaiting Trial' etc., and lastly, the prisoner's religion. The hallways were filled with noise and clamour. I thought about Muskogee and how I had initially thought that it was a place of racket and uproar. Compared to this, Muskogee seemed like a place of serenity and stillness. Here I was surrounded by chaos. There was shouting, screaming and cursing. I was told that prisoners had been known to set fire to their cells or their mattresses and it wasn't unusual to have someone try to commit suicide. After five days I was moved to Foil House. My cell-mate was a young man who chain smoked. He didn't bathe and ate his food with his unwashed hands. I tried to pray and meditate but couldn't concentrate because my stomach started rolling and bile kept coming up in my throat. I requested an audience with the governor of the house and told him that I believed my civil rights were being violated by being forced to share a cell with a smoker. He stared at me in a bored, vacant way and proceeded to lecture me on my civil rights. He was not a great governor and had no intention of doing anything. Once I realized that, I repeated that he was violating my civil rights and endangering my health. If he wouldn't do anything about that I would have to inform my attorneys of what was happening. He paused and said, "We'll have you moved to the next available single." "Thank you, sir." I said. "That's all," he responded. "You can go now." After about a week a single cell became available on my floor. I informed the head guard that I had been promised by the governor that I would be first in line for the single. "Well," said the head guard, "I'm afraid that cell has been promised to another member of your fine upstanding community." "But the governor promised it to me," I repeated. "The governor does not run this wing, I run this wing and you will get the cell when I decide and not a moment sooner." "Well we'll just see about that," I told him. The head guard made an apoplectic face and the other guard behind the desk raised his eyebrows. I stood there and just stared at them. "You do not frighten me," I implied with that stare. Finally, I turned and slowly walked away. "Will you look at the nerve of that one!" said the guard behind the desk. "Bloody other!" muttered the head guard. "Bloody other!" Shortly after, I was moved into a single.

I lived in that single through the spring and summer, for eight months as the wheels of justice slowly turned. During those eight months I learned a lot. I learned what 'cutting the beef' meant, a term to indicate someone had tried to slit their wrists. There was a lot of that happening during my time there. I learned what it was like to have my cell ransacked and to have my clothes strewn about. I learned what it was to have my personal letters rifled through and read. I learned what it was to be taken to court once a month while chained within a tiny cubicle, in the back of a truck. I learned what it was to stand in that court, month after month, and then be told that the prosecutor was 'not ready to proceed against you'. I learned to have patience, how to wait and how to make myself ready for whatever was to happen. The barrister that Joe Rice had originally engaged had to excuse himself because he knew one of the witnesses in my case. In the meantime, I had heard from the 'travellers' in prison that if I could get him, Arthur Harvey was the man to have. I asked Joe if he had heard of, or knew of, Arthur. The answer was yes. He doubted we could get him because he was the number one of the top three barristers in Northern Ireland. He was very sought after, but he said, "I will ask him." Joe sent my file over to Arthur; a few days later he was happy to find out that Arthur had accepted. Joe told me that he had said, "Here is a man I can help. I have studied the facts and the evidence and it is patently clear to me that this is not a case about justice; this is a case about politics." When I met him, he shook my hand. "Mr Ross," he said, "I have one request before proceeding with your case. I want to make it perfectly clear that you and I are not friends; you are my client. You will address me as Mr Harvey at all times and I shall address you as Mr Ross, is that understood?" "Yes, Mr Harvey," I responded. "Thank you." "My pleasure indeed, Mr Ross. My pleasure indeed!"

20

NORTHERN IRELAND AND
MAGHABERRY PRISON

uskogee had the capacity to house twenty-two people in my unit. In my new environment, Maghaberry, there were over a hundred inmates. Because of the monotony of prison, everyone was always interested in the 'new man'. When I was in the exercise yard, I found I would be periodically stopped by an inmate passing me at one spot and then by someone else further along my walk. They would ask me questions about myself. Some of these men I liked, and some of them had energies that I didn't want to be around. I would be polite but did not encourage discussions. I met a lot of different sorts of people including a few political prisoners from the Real I.R.A. and the Protestant paramilitaries. The I.R.A (Irish Republican Army) is made up of three factions; the Real I.R.A, the Continuity I.R.A. and the Provo I.R.A. There was one particularly well educated and dedicated man, the first one I met early on, who was in the Real I.R.A. I was under the impression that all they would be interested in talking about was politics, history, guns and revenge. I realized once again how naive I was as he and the others never spoke of their organization or their political beliefs. They spoke about life, love, their families and their friends. They spoke about fishing, traveling, poetry and having a pint with their friends. They were philosophers of a sort who did not once complain about being victims of oppression or injustice. They were men dedicated to their cause of bringing about a unified Ireland no longer under British rule. They talked about how grateful they were to breathe fresh air and enjoy the afternoon sun in the exercise yard. They taught me many things, not by their words, but by the example of their actions. I met another man on my first day there and as he walked by my cell, he glanced in and noticed my books. He asked to borrow some. I was happy to accommodate him. I usually went in the exercise yard in the mornings but not so much in the evening. One day, as I walked around the yard, I noticed a group of men all gathered together in one area. I thought that was odd but continued on my walk. As I passed one particular individual, sitting on a step, holding a mug of tea, he said to me, "You stole my granny's money!" I ignored him and continued walking. The next time the circle brought me past him he repeated, "You stole my granny's money!" I ignored him again. He did this a number of times until finally I stopped and looked directly at him. "Do you have a problem with me?" I asked. "You're a liar and a thief. You stole my granny's money!" "That's not true," I said. "It's not true because I am not a liar and I am not a thief. It's not true because I never stole anybody's money. It's not true because your granny did not have any money in the first place." He looked back at me and then down at his tea. The steam was rising from the mug. He then looked back up at me and I knew in that moment what he was planning to do. Scalding was a common thing here. "Go for it. Go for it and see where your head will end up." A sudden silence descended. Everyone in the yard stopped whatever they were doing to watch me and the prisoner with the steaming cup of tea in his hand. "I will scald you," he threatened. "You can do anything you want," I replied. "But I have learned that all actions have consequences. I think it is only fair to warn you that I have just spent fourteen and a half months in a jail in Oklahoma. Do you know where Oklahoma is? It's in the wild west of America. The men that I lived with there would have eaten you for breakfast, so if you want to come after me, go for it and see what will happen to you." "I will bloody well scald you," he said again. "Go ahead," I said. "You can always try, but remember, all actions have consequences!" My hands were trembling so I hid them in my pockets. Every cell in my body was charged with fear and terror. I didn't want to fight but I knew they were testing me to see what I was made of, and where I fit in the pack. I knew if I wanted to survive, I had better be solid. He must have seen the determination in my face. My eyes never left his so he thought better of continuing. He looked away, and then to the left as the confrontation eased the others walked away.

As the days and weeks passed, I knew I had to create a different environment for myself again, like I had in Muskogee. I wanted to be of service so I began to observe those around me. Slowly I began to have discussions with other prisoners whom I thought would be receptive. I began to tell them my story and I listened to theirs. I prayed with some of them and wrote letters for others. I sought out those who I knew were thinking of 'cutting the beef'. I talked to them and encouraged them to speak about what was going on with them. Sometimes I felt I was helping, other times I wasn't so sure. I just knew that listening to them helped me. Elvis was one man I was able to help, indirectly. He was innocent and everyone knew it. He had taken the rap for his wife and he was an alcoholic. He also took pills, whatever ones no one wanted like Valium, Prozac, and the like. One day word came to me that he was going to 'cut the beef'—commit suicide. I talked to him and said, "Don't do anything until we talk again after lockdown. Just wait." I was waiting for a particular guard to come on duty, who was a good guy. Unfortunately, he wasn't on duty that afternoon so, I had no choice but to talk to the guard who was working. He was a deacon in the church and I explained everything to him and I told him that Elvis was thinking of 'cutting the beef'. He went directly into Elvis's cell and started lecturing him about, 'If you do the crime, you do the time.' Instead of helping, he just made things worse. I was so upset. I had misjudged him. He did not have an ounce of compassion for this man. That evening the nice guard came on duty, a man who had been a policeman in another life and I told him what was going on. He said to leave it with him that he would take care of it. Within a short time, men in white coats arrived and took Elvis away. When he was returned a week later he had joined AA (Alcoholics Anonymous). Two months later Elvis was released.

The youngest guard in Foil House was different from the

others. He was sympathetic and courteous. He treated me, and others, like human beings. One day, I asked him if I could have permission to visit another wing in the prison to pray and do some healing work with a young man who was thinking of 'cutting the beef' and to my surprise he granted me permission. I worked with this young man and then with several others in a third wing, over a period of about four weeks. Then one day, as I was making my way down to the other wing, I heard my name called. When I reported to the front desk, I saw that my old friend, the head guard, was back from vacation. "Where in the bloody hell do you think you're going?" "I am going down to the other wing," I responded. "What businesses have you down there?" he asked. "I am going down there to pray with some of the men," I explained. "You've no authority to do that." "But I do, sir," I said. "I've been given permission." "Nobody's given you any bloody permission!" "Yes, they have," I responded. I told him about my friend, the young guard. "That means bollocks to me," he said. He handed me a slip of paper. "Fill this out and apply to the governor for permission and then we'll see what kind of permission you'll have." I filled out the form and the next morning I was called before the governor of Lagan House. He was filling in for the governor of Foil House. (There were eight cell blocks to a house and each house had a governor.) He read the request and asked me how long I had been doing this. After I told him, he asked me if I didn't realize that it was against the rules. "Cannot these men pray with the chaplain on Sunday?" he asked. "There are six other days in the week," I responded. "Any one of those days can be a day when one of these young men has a spiritual crisis. What are they to do then,

Governor? Are they only to have spiritual crisis/comfort and sustenance once a week?" "What are you playing at?" he questioned. "I'm not playing at anything, sir. Your guards are bullies; some are passive-aggressive; some treat the men with no respect. If praying with some of the men can prevent them from 'cutting the beef', then surely it cannot be against the rules." "What guards are bullies? Give me names." "You are the governor, sir. Are you telling me you do not know the men who serve under you? Are you telling me you do not know what goes on in your own house? Are you telling me you do not know your own men? Is that what you are telling me, sir, that you do not know which men are passive-aggressive and such?" He looked at me in shock. I stood there facing him on my own two feet, looking him in the eye. I have learned by now that there are many ways to bring change. "I promise you I will take care of this, in my own way," he said. "But I need names so that I can look into it." I didn't like the thought of naming names. "I will give you two names of guards," I told him. "I will give you two names of the worst offenders and then I will watch with interest what you do with that information." "You're quite an unusual man," he said. "I don't know about that, but I do know you need to get to know your men and what goes on in here."

A week later the two guards were removed from wing duty and sent to visitor and security detail and I was transferred to Lagan House. Life in Lagan House was a paradise compared to Foil House as here the guards were decent and human. They treated the men with respect and asked only for respect in return. Shortly after I was there, I learned that most of the guards in Foil House came from the old Crumlin Road jail. They had a history of prejudice, abuse and intolerance. I also had another incident with the prison guards at the court. One evening when I was being brought back to Maghaberry Prison, the officer came into the cell where I was being held at the courthouse, put me in handcuffs and started dragging me behind him, which I resisted. I said to him, "I am not a dog, so stop dragging me. Just tell me where you want me to go and I will go." As this was all happening, we reached a point where we were in an island where gates opened in three directions, a square of about ten feet by ten feet. Another officer was there, who was the officer in charge within the court and he asked what was going on. The first officer told him I was resisting being pulled by him. His response to me was, "In here you are nothing. We can do anything we want with you!" He made a movement to put his hand in his pants pocket where it looked like he had a baton. At that moment I felt an explosion in my head resulting in a major headache which was so bad, that when I got back to Maghaberry I asked to see a doctor and made a complaint. When I got to my cell, it turned out that some people from an organization called Prison Visitors, who looked into prisoner complaints, were on our wing. They came to see me where I told them what had happened. During the telling of the story I started crying; I did not even know why I was crying. The Prison Visitors were so concerned by all of this that they came back again the following day, to see me. I saw the doctor for these headaches for about the next three weeks. My attorney, Joe Rice, of course made a formal complaint to the prison governor, also expressing my fears that, although I was afraid of this officer, I would have to see him each day, during my trial, which was coming up shortly. The great thing that came out of all of this was, that the way we were taken to, and from, the transport changed. We now had one hand, handcuffed to the hand of a prison officer, who walked along with us. This also brought about a big change between the officer in charge at the court, and myself. We talked and he often just walked with me to the transport with no handcuffs. Needless to say, my medical file went missing just in case I sued.

21

THE TRIALS

n the end, I had to go through three trials in Northern Ireland. The first one ended in a hung jury. This was a very intense and emotional time for me, day-after-day in court. The trial lasted six weeks and during the first ten days my name was not even mentioned. Mr Harvey, the Barrister now representing me, said he wondered what was up until he actually heard my name spoken. He was starting to think that this trial was about someone else. Several witnesses spoke about their investments with International Investments stating they knew that risks were involved and then some of the investment brokers got on the stand and committed perjury. We were able to prove this through documentation provided to us by Billy Flynn. This documentation was filed in the Gibraltar court by Colm Allen, a Dublin Barrister who represented Frank Murray and some of the Investment brokers. In their sworn affidavits they stated facts that were not true. It appeared they had been prepared by Colm Allen. It became clear, under cross examination, these men were committing perjury, but nothing happened to them. The liquidator, James Galliano, under cross-examination, could not answer questions about where monies from the asset disposals ended up. This left me dumb-founded, as the paperwork clearly stated that the assets were disposed of, but there was no paper trail of the monies. Also, after the trial, we found out why Frank Murray was not prosecuted in 1991. He had worked for James Galliano, the liquidator, and had been involved in the disposal of some of the aforementioned assets. Because of this, the liquidator would not agree to give evidence against Frank Murray. The only person whose recounting of the events was even close to matching my testimony, was Ronnie Vincent's; everyone else's was fabricated. At one point, when I was on the stand, the judge asked me how I knew so much about the liquidation and other events. I replied that I got it all from the paperwork provided by the prosecution. There was no doubt, the paperwork left a lot of unanswered questions, but it also clearly did answer a fair amount as well. As to the unanswered ones, Mr Harvey was quite brilliant in asking the questions that no one wanted to answer. Finally, the time came for the jury to be sent to the jury room to deliberate and agree on a verdict.

It ended with a hung jury, a jury of my peers who were from the Belfast area. I was told later that two of the ladies on the jury revealed that because I was from the south of Ireland they thought that I had to be guilty. I also had to be guilty because, in their opinion, the Royal Ulster Constabulary would never arrest a man from the south of Ireland, if he wasn't guilty. Another lady also had her own opinion of why I was guilty. She cast her vote as non-guilty on Friday when the jury was polled, but changed her vote to guilty by the following Monday morning when the jury was polled again. As the verdict was announced I just stood there in shock. We had all expected a verdict of not guilty. Now I would have to stand trial once more. The judge turned to me and said, "I suppose you wish to apply for bail?" "Yes, you're Lordship," I answered. "Yes, I would." The prosecutor objected. He stated that I had not been proven innocent by any means and that I should be returned to Maghaberry to await confirmation from the Crown that there would be a retrial. "I don't think so," responded the judge. "If this man had appeared before me six weeks ago seeking bail, I don't know what my decision would have been. But with everything I have heard here, over the past six weeks, I know this man does not need to be in jail. I will call a brief recess and give you time to consult your superiors." Twenty minutes later the court reconvened and I was granted bail! My sister Catherine put up the deeds to her home. My friend, Jack Moriarty, posted an additional twenty-thousand dollars. Two days later I was released into my sister's custody after I surrendered my passport. For the first time in two years I was a free man! I was released to live in the Republic of Ireland, which was outside the jurisdiction of the Northern Ireland courts. I returned to the place of my birth, to the place from which I had run away, so many years ago. It was ironic. The road had led me back to the beginning. I felt great, but I was also nervous. I knew a lot could happen in two years. I was sure the outside world would have changed in unexpected ways. Still, excitement overrode my apprehension, hands down. As we left the parking lot, the first thing I asked my sister was to find us a place, where I could have a salmon steak and a glass of wine for dinner. I hadn't had either in two years! A little while later we crossed the border into Southern Ireland. Soon after crossing the border, we stopped in Dundalk for a meal. The salmon tasted wonderful. I savoured every bite as I enjoyed my meal in the peace and quiet of the restaurant. This was a far cry from the chow line I had been standing in the night before. It was such a pleasure to linger over the meal and not be confined to a timetable, or hear orders being blasted out over the loud speaker. Later, when I went to bed that night, I was filled with gratitude to the Universe, to my God, Mother Mary, all the Masters, and to my guides. For the first time, in a long, long while, I was able to sleep in a room by myself, on a comfortable bed, with soft sheets. I didn't have to go to sleep with the sound of the sliders shutting, and get up to the sound of them opening. Sliders was the name in prison of the sliding doors that were between wings or sections of the prison. Now, instead, I could simply open, or shut, a door; or not, if I so chose. The freedom to walk anywhere, anytime, or to feel the sun on my face in the morning or afternoon and not be restricted to a specific time for a limited period was so precious. I also felt such relief not having to watch my back all of the time. I didn't realize how strongly I had had to steel myself against the unseen dangers in prison until I heard a car honking soon after being released from prison and I nearly jumped out of my skin. I was shocked at my reaction. I hadn't expected to have such a subconscious response to such an ordinary sound. I realized it was an old response that was no longer necessary in my new surroundings. I was once more in control of my own life, although I wasn't totally free yet. I still had another trial ahead of me. One of the conditions of being out on bail was that, once a week, every week, I had to make the six-hour trip across the border to report to the police in Newry, Northern Ireland. After a month of doing this, I applied to the court to have it changed to once per month, pleading the difficulty of traveling that distance. In the meantime, a friend of mine, Simon Peter, came to visit me in Cork. I had met Simon Peter twice in Oklahoma when he had come to visit and speak at the Church's annual conference in 1996 and we had remained friends. We had met again in Seattle where we did some ceremonies together. During his visit to me in Ireland, in the early summer of 2000, he mentioned he was going to be offering a sacred site tour to Scotland in a few months and invited me to join him. I first had to get permission from the RUC (Royal Ulster Constabulary) inspector in charge of my case. He was able to grant it because the travels would be within the jurisdiction of the United Kingdom. That trip went a long way to helping me get back to normal and to heal in some small ways. As we travelled through Scotland, Simon Peter and I, talked about my future and what I planned to do once the trials were finally over. He suggested I might want to offer sacred site tours as well, as I was suited to it, along with doing my healing work. This made perfect sense to me. One of the responsibilities that I took on at Sparrow Hawk was making all the arrangements for the tours they offered and looking after all the logistics. I had also participated in some of the tours so I knew what was involved. Peter also suggested that I could offer my Divine Feminine Emotional Healing workshops as well. Again, this made sense, as I had already been doing healing work while at Sparrow Hawk. It seemed that my time there was well-spent in many ways, and would serve me well now. Both ideas seemed promising but, before I could act on them, I had to wait for the trial to be over. For that to happen, it first had to start! It wasn't until almost a year later that trial number two started. The day before the trial began, I had a meeting with my attorney, Joe Rice, and my Senior Council (Barrister), Mr Harvey. Mr Harvey told me, quite clearly, that I was going to be found guilty, this time. He said, "You can't win. This time you have a judge who will find you guilty even if the prosecutor can't and you won't have a jury of your peers." This jury didn't come from Belfast, but rather from the small town of Carrick Fergus. They were decent law-abiding citizens who were young. They would do exactly what the judge instructed them to do. The trial lasted just over four weeks. Some of the witnesses from the first trial could not be found for this one, but it was very much a repeat performance of the first one. The same evidence within the affidavits filed in Gibraltar by Colm Allen, was in play. From the beginning, the judge Lord Justice McCollum manipulated and twisted the evidence, so much so, that he and Mr Harvey, exchanged harsh words at the end of day one. Mr Harvey informed Lord Justice McCollum that if he planned to follow that line of inquiry we would need six weeks for forensic accountants to investigate the accounting procedures pertaining to the information provided. The following morning Lord Justice McCollum arrived back in court, informing the court that we were not going to continue along that line of inquiry as it was outside the scope of the charges. This was a very emotionally charged and stressful time for me because, I realised that the judge was gunning for me. The case continued as finally each barrister made his submission. First, the prosecutor told the jury why I was guilty; that took three hours. Then, Mr Harvey spent a full day telling them why I was not. Finally, the judge took a day and a half to sum up. Unfortunately for me, he instructed them in such a way that they had no alternative but to find me guilty. "I have a hard time believing the witness," he informed them. He was talking about one particular witness's testimony who was testifying for the prosecution. The jury listened to the judge's every word, with full attention. They were decent people. They believed the judge as he rambled on, talking about events that had not happened and evidence that had not been presented in the trial. They are naïve, I thought. I knew what it was to be naïve. I had been there. I sat there in the dock, a male and female officer on either side of me, listening with resignation. The female officer became very upset with the way the judge was presenting his summary. During the time he was doing so, she remarked, on several occasions, what he was saying was not in the evidence. Her male counterpart kept asking her to be quiet. Finally, she turned to me after some outlandish statement the judge had made and said, "At this moment I am ashamed to be Northern Irish. It is men like this judge who make me ashamed. He has no regard for justice." The judge, of course, was a Lord Justice McCollum, so when he then sent the jury out for deliberation, Mr Harvey jumped to his feet and protested. He told the Lord Justice that he had shown a blatant disregard for my rights. He informed him that he had committed nineteen major violations of my rights along with numerous lesser ones. After two hours of Mr Harvey detailing the violations committed in his summing up to the court, the Lord

Justice turned to the prosecutor. "What do you have to say about Mr Harvey's allegations that I have violated the defendant's rights with regards to Mr Vincent's and Mr Ross's evidence? Were they as Mr Harvey states?" "Well, they were substantially the same, Your Honour." "What do you have to say about his other allegations?" "It is not for me to comment, Your Lordship," commented the prosecutor and so reluctantly the Lord Justice McCollum called the jury back into the court room. When the jury returned the Lord Justice looked at me and then back at the jury. "While you have been out in the jury room pondering the evidence, Mr Harvey has been on his feet for the past two hours telling me how I violated his client's rights with nineteen major violations and numerous lesser ones. Now what I have to say to you is that you will ignore all previous instruction I have given you with regards to the difference in Mr Vincent's evidence and Mr Ross's, as it appears that their evidence was substantially the same. As regards the other points brought up by Mr Harvey, you are to make your own determination." Of course, the Lord Justice McCollum did not state what the other eighteen points were, so it was impossible for the jury to know what he was talking about and so the decent law-abiding citizens of the jury looked solemnly at the Lord Justice as they filed back out of the court. They did not look at me. The following day they returned with their verdict. They found me guilty. The wonderful Lord Justice took delight in giving me a lecture before sentencing me to thirty months. He maligned my character and said what a disgrace I was. I sat there dumbfounded even though I was prepared for this. I was taken to Maghaberry Prison to be processed and told that my medical file had gone missing. This didn't surprise me. I had been warned that it would go missing in order to prevent me from suing the Prison Service for the incident that took place before my first trial with the prison officers at the court. I no longer cared about that; I no longer wanted revenge; I only wanted justice. True, I was back in prison, sentenced to thirty months, but I knew I would be released immediately. I knew that the combined time I had served in the States and Northern Ireland exceeded the time for which I was sentenced, so in effect, I had already served my time. Still, in Northern Ireland prisoners had to serve five additional days for the Queen. I did not care about the Queen or her corrupt government: I didn't mind spending another five days. I thought I would serve those five days, then I would appeal the verdict. However, the next morning I had a surprise. The governor informed me that I still had five and a half months to serve. "No, that isn't true," I told him. "I've only the five days. I've only the five days for the Queen." "No, no, no," he responded. "Your time in America will not be taken into account. You have five and a half months left to serve, and the five days for the Queen." I found out the judge in my case ruled against allowing my time in Muskogee to stand. I called Joe Rice who sent a friend of his to talk with the judge, who responded that he was not allowing my time in America to be taken into account, but if I wanted to petition the court to include that time I would have to go through the proper channels, knowing well that this would take several months. Of course, by now, my attorneys had lodged an appeal with the court based on the nineteen civil rights violations of the previous judge. It was an unbelievable political mess that offered no justice. I felt totally devastated but that wasn't the end of it. There was more bad news. "You are being moved to Magilligan Prison in County Londonderry." I protested. It was quite a ways away and I knew it would be too far for anyone to come and visit me. Once again my protests fell on deaf ears as I went through the familiar routine of being admitted. Later I sat there in my cell thinking of all that had happened as I tried to fathom things out. I wondered what the point of all that I had learned and experienced through all of this saga was. What could it be if it was only to bring me back once again to a prison cell? I was moved within a couple of days to Magilligan Prison, a wild and beautiful place in the Northwest of Ireland. Here, the wind swept with gale forces so powerful that not even a tree could slow it down. The food was better there than in Maghaberry Prison. Some of the officers were nice, while others were not. We were locked down a lot there, so I had lots of time to ponder the events of my life. After about five days I came to the realization that I was not going anywhere until I resolved the issues (within myself) with my friend, the Lord Justice. This process took me three days. Finally, in my consciousness, I was able to hold him in my arms and thank him for being an actor on the stage of my life bringing me to a greater awareness about forgiveness for others and myself. Once I was able to do that with genuine feeling, I approached Mother Mary in prayer and said, "Now I want a miracle in my life." I did this at about 10:00 am: around 3:00 pm my cell door opened. I was handed two paper sacks and told to pack my stuff. "Ross, you are going to Belfast in the morning." I asked what for and he answered, "I have no idea!" I asked if could phone my attorney. He said sure, so I called my attorney and as luck would have it I got a hold of Joe Rice. I asked him what was going on and he said, "We have no idea!" All he could tell me was that they had got a phone call from the Lord Chief Justice's office asking them to have me in court the next day for a special sitting of the Court. "Now you know as much as I do, except that I can tell you that your leave to appeal has been granted." The following morning two prison guards and I left bright and early for the few hours journey to Belfast. When we got there I spoke with Joe Rice and Mr Harvey, but they told me they still knew nothing. Finally we entered the courtroom, which was empty because no one knew there was a special sitting. Shortly after we entered, the Lord Chief Justice, who was one of the three most senior judges in Northern Ireland, and the Deputy Lord Chief Justice appeared and took their places on the bench. The Lord Chief Justice spoke to Mr Harvey and said, "Mr Harvey, we have a bail application from you on behalf of Mr Ross, which was filed with the request for leave to appeal." "Yes your Lordship," Mr Harvey responded. Now we knew why I had been called there, but still didn't understand why there was a special sitting. Mr Harvey started to give all the reasons why I should be granted bail when the Lord Chief Justice put up his hand and said, "Mr Harvey, what were the conditions of Mr Ross's previous bail?" Mr Harvey told him and the Lord Chief Justice spoke to the prosecutor and asked if they had any objections. He responded no, and the R.U.C. were neutral as always. The Lord Chief Justice spoke with the Deputy Lord Chief Justice, after which he said bail was granted on the same conditions. All of this happened within fifteen minutes and once again I was freed on bail. Before we left the court Mr Harvey requested transcripts of the trial, which the Lord Chief Justice ordered. Once again, we were back in a waiting game, waiting for a date to be set early in the following year as we were just less than two months from Christmas. What a feeling of joy and gratitude I felt as I left the court knowing that there had to be justice some place in Northern Ireland. In spite of everything, in spite of the fact that nothing that had happened so far gave me any reason to feel that, I knew there was justice to be had. I had absolute faith, blind faith you could say, as I went back down to Dublin and West Cork. The months passed and I made my monthly visits to Newry and to the courts in Belfast inquiring about the appeal. Finally in July, The Lord Chief Justice ran out of patience with the court system and the hold-up on the trial transcripts of the court. All of this served the purpose of the prosecution that was forever offering me deals, suggesting I plead to something, anything, even parking tickets, for time served, to make everything go away. My response to Mr Harvey, who would bring me these deals, never varied. "Why are you bothering me with these deals? Have I not told you hell will freeze over before I take a deal?" He would answer, "I know that, but I am duty bound to offer you these deals." While I had been waiting for things to proceed, I had been busy doing healing work and counselling, so the time wasn't wasted but I really needed to get my life back on track. Finally, at the end of July the transcripts arrived and the Lord Chief Justice set a date in early September for the trial, which was great news. Just before the appeal, the prosecutor offered his final deal. If I agreed to plead guilty to any one of the charges I would be released for time served. I would receive a letter from the United States State Department stating that, by pleading guilty, nothing would happen to my U.S. citizenship. My U.S. passport would be returned and I would be free to come and go. "What do you want to do, Mr Ross?" asked Mr Harvey. "You know my answer, Mr Harvey. I will not plead guilty to something I did not do." "Is that your final answer, Mr Ross?" he asked. "Yes, Mr Harvey. That is my final answer." "That's what I thought, Mr Ross. That's what I thought." I stood in the Appeals Court before three of the highest ranking judges in Northern Ireland, The Lord Chief Justice, the Deputy Lord Chief Justice and the Chief Justice. The appeal began with Mr Harvey outlining what he considered to be the court's violations of my civil rights, focusing on the testimony of Ronnie Vincent and how the Lord Justice had totally miss-stated Ronnie's evidence to the jury. He then went on to mention the other violations; his presentation took one and a half days. At the end of it, the Lord Chief Justice could only come up with one inconsequential question. I found this whole process fascinating to watch. This time I had a side seat with no prison officers beside me. From there, I could see Mr Harvey's face and his expressions, as well as those of the judges. It was very different from the previous trials where I was seated behind Mr Harvey in the dock. Finally it was the prosecutor's turn. Mr Craney started with his usual assumptions, lies and evasions as in the previous two trials. As I watched this, I was captivated because, within a short time of Mr Craney's starting to speak, I noticed Mr Harvey getting redder and redder in the face. The prosecutor continued to ramble and mislead the court with blatant untruths until finally Mr Harvey jumped up and shouted, "My Lords, I must protest! It is this kind of talk and innuendo that brought us here. There is no basis of fact or truth in what my learned friend is saying!" I thought, oh my God we are sunk and gone forever. My understanding was that Mr Harvey could not speak while Mr Craney was making his submission. On that point I am still not sure, but at that time, it seemed that what was done, was done. The Lord Chief Justice thanked Mr Harvey who then sat down. From that moment on the court took on a whole new tone. The deputy Lord Chief Justice started grilling Mr Craney about each of his statements and where it was in the evidence. Finally, as the day was coming to a close, the Lord Chief Justice addressed the prosecutor. "Mr Craney, when you arrive tomorrow morning, can you please have your argument in bullet points so that we may ask you some questions?" "Yes, you're Lordship," said the prosecutor. The next morning the prosecutor addressed the court, reading from his bullet points. He quickly went off on one tangent after another. The Chief Justice who had not spoken up to this point suddenly piped up. "Where is this in the evidence?" "It's not actually in the evidence, Your Lordship," answered the prosecutor. "But it's what the witness intended to say." "How do I know that is what the witness intended to say? It is not anywhere in this transcript." This continued for over two hours. Each time the prosecutor would level an accusation against me, the Chief Justice called him to task and required that he cite specific evidence supporting the charge. The prosecutor was not able to respond with anything but conjecture and supposition until finally he rested his case. I was totally blown away watching this man, the Chief Justice. For over two hours he never looked at a note.

However he could recite, verbatim, from the transcript of the previous trial in which I was found guilty. Whereas the prosecutor, Mr Craney, kept going off on tangents to throw people off, distracting them from what was really in the transcripts. It was fascinating to watch. The Lord Chief Justice looked me directly in the eye. "Well, Mr Ross, I presume you wish to make a request for bail?" "Yes, your Honour," I responded. "Mr Ross, do you realize that you have stretched this court?" "Yes, your Honour," I said. He repeated it again. And I again said, "yes Your Honour" after a pause, that appeared to last forever, "Mr Ross, it is the custom here in Northern Ireland that while one is waiting for a decision from the Appeals Court that one goes back to prison. However, I see no useful purpose being served in this instance. I just want you to fully realize how you have stretched this court." I couldn't say anything. I nodded my head up and down as I looked at him. It was as if there was no one else in the court, or in the world, for that matter but he and I as we looked directly into one another's eyes. I saw compassion in his and was able to glimpse the depth of his humanity; he also seemed to look into the depths of my soul. It felt like a very strong spiritual connection happened between us. He held my gaze for a few seconds more and then he said, "It will take six weeks for us to reach our decision, but don't worry, we will give you plenty of notice to get yourself back here for the decision. Bail will continue with the same provision," he said without taking his eyes from me. "This court is now dismissed." With that decision I found myself going back to Dublin where I stayed with friends to wait out the six weeks, grateful that I did not have to go back to Maghaberry Prison. That was an unexpected gift. The one belief that kept me going through all of this, which I came to see as my vision quest, was that there had to be justice found some place in Northern Ireland. I had little reason to believe this because the court system there did not have a great reputation but still, I was sure of this, and my interaction with the Lord Chief Justice proved it to be so. I felt that I had finally met a man of honour. I certainly did not meet men of honour in the United States court system.

In the end, the decision took a little longer than six weeks to be reached. The Lord Chief Justice apologized as he had had the flu. The decision of the court was that my conviction and sentence should be set aside and stricken from the records as the case against me was based on innuendo. The Lord Chief Justice wished me well and that was it! It was finally over. I was exonerated. The relief that flowed through me was astonishing. I was so happy to have all this behind me and also grateful for all that I had learned on this vision quest. I came through this a better and stronger person, albeit with a number of deep emotional scars. I experienced a beautiful moment of gratitude as I shook hands with Mr Harvey and Joe Rice, both of whom were elated. The reason that Mr Harvey had taken my case after reading the book of evidence was borne out. He had said, back then, "Here is a man I can help," and he was right. Outside the court I met my friend Jim McCarthy. We were both in a state of euphoria that it was finally over. I could now close that chapter of my life and open the page to a new one. We drove to Dublin, stopping on the way to make phone calls to let people know the results, although it wasn't necessary. The decision had been on the radio and TV so most people were already aware of the situation. At this point in time my heart was so full of love, gratitude and appreciation. I was totally connected within with Mother Mary who was as always my guide and companion and who had held my hand at each step of this vision quest. I could feel the power and the vibration of the divine mother celebrating with me as I walked down the street feeling fully empowered.

✳

PART TWO

LIVING THE INNER DIVINE WISDOM

22

SACRED MYSTICAL JOURNEYS

Jim asked me what I intended to do now that the trial was over and I was a free man. I said my intent was to return to the States. A very good friend of mine, Austin Delaney, provided the necessary funds to set me on my journey. I gave some thought to where I wanted to live and had decided on Dallas as it had a big international airport. I also had a good friend there who offered me a place to stay. Also, from there, I could easily fly anywhere, which was going to be important because I had decided I was going to start a spiritual tour company. Over all, it seemed a good place to settle and a good plan. Initially, I arranged tours to Ireland, Scotland and England. At first, in the lean times, for my air travel I flew on vouchers that a flight attendant friend gave me. I travelled to India and Sri Lanka with Simon Peter in 2002. In conjunction with Simon Peter, I added these countries to my tours in 2003, as well as a few other places. It was quite hard in the beginning. I was learning about how to organize all the logistics of the tours as well as how to meet the varied needs of different individual travellers. It took time, but I was able to reach a point where I could anticipate and be prepared for most of their needs. Over the years, I kept adding different tours through my guidance from Mother Mary. Mother Mary has always been my special guide. I always feel divinely inspired when she urges me to take on yet another destination. Today, I offer sacred site tours to over sixteen countries and I am not done yet. Arranging tours takes a tremendous amount of time and work. In order to be able to offer the best kind of spiritual experiences, means I have to do a lot of research. In setting up the logistics for the tours, I had to also set up a website, advertise, and find the right type of person to answer calls and make the bookings. I had to learn how to get the best rates from the hotels and bus companies. I needed to scout out restaurants which offered good wholesome food, along with a diverse enough menu, to accommodate most tastes. In Ireland, I spent thirty-two days driving around visiting sacred sites deciding which ones I should include in the tour. This process continued as I explored sites in England and Scotland, followed by France, Turkey, Guatemala, Peru, India, Sri Lanka, Egypt, Israel, Italy, Malta, Thailand, Cambodia and Myanmar, Greece, and then Malta/Sicily, my new addition, to the tours. I also had to deal with the after-effects of having been in jail and prison. Even though I had been exonerated, I still had lots of challenges every time I entered the United States. Every time I showed my passport, my arrest record kept coming up. It took about five years to get that sorted out, during which time, I missed many a flight being detained because of my arrest record. These were nerve-wracking experiences. Some of the immigration officers were very nasty in their treatment of me, going through my luggage, wallet, and briefcase as well as asking very personal questions. In the end, I learned that the quickest way for me to get through immigration was to do it through Dublin, Ireland as the U.S. Immigration people there got to know me well. They knew where to go to resolve the issue. Otherwise, I knew I would have a two or three-hour wait while the staff tried to find the right people with the right answers. Finally, with the help of an immigration officer in Dublin, I found out who to contact in Washington D.C. It took about six months to get it all resolved, but now I can walk through immigration with ease. Still, with this and everything else, it took me at least a year to feel safe on the streets. I felt insecure because of fears of being attacked, flashbacks of being constantly on guard in prison along with the hassle with immigration. Finally I went for some counselling and also saw an expert on post-traumatic stress who helped me tremendously, so I could relax. I had to deal with health issues, too, that developed because of my time in prison. It took years. The number of tours I offered grew. I found myself spending about six to seven months every year traveling. When I was home, I focused on my other passion which was offering Divine Feminine Emotional Healing workshops. What is a sacred journey! A friend of mine described it as follows:

Food for thought!—Pilgrims or Tourists

We are told we should be pilgrims in life, but instead we have become tourists. Pilgrims are on a special journey. Every part of it has meaning -the setbacks, the frustrations, as well as the joys. Tourists are out to enjoy life, to seek pleasure, fun or just rest. Pilgrims carry little with them, just enough for their needs. Tourists are burdened with possessions and are always anxious about losing them. Pilgrims stay as long as they need to be in a place. Tourists have schedules to keep and are always rushing on. Pilgrims are humble, open to people and experiences. Tourists are arrogant, they know what they want, and they'll see it, do it, and find it. Pilgrims share what they have. Tourists never have quite enough. Pilgrims are changed by their journey. Tourists are always a little bit disappointed—it is never quite as good as they had hoped. Lord, help us to be pilgrims in life—not just tourists.

Isabelle Kingston

A sacred journey is really a spiritual intensive for the period of the journey. This spiritual intensive begins the moment you make your reservation and start packing. It is a journey whereby each person learns about group consciousness. As we travel on these journeys, we are weaving a collective spiritual tapestry. As one quests each day, they are immersed in the matrix of each sacred site where the ancient vibrational energy of the site meets up and interacts with the energy of the now within each person. For one to reach a higher vibrational state, one must lift up one's consciousness. When one is able to lift their consciousness, it is at this point that each person has their own shift in consciousness, their own spiritual/mystical experience at a particular site. It may be the vibration of the site itself which could initiate these experiences, or it could be the meditation, ceremony, or rituals we do at the sites that starts the process. The unique energy of each site opens one up to different new

178

initiations, experiences and awareness. Each challenge one encounters on a sacred journey, whether it be issues with someone else on the tour, the food, or whatever it is being mirrored back to them, is something they need to look at in their life. These challenges are engineered by our Souls, not to punish us in any way, but to bring us opportunities for soul growth and healing as there is no separation between each of us and our soul; we are one. The intensity of the journey can continue for many weeks after the tour ends as one processes the many conscious and unconscious vibrational changes taking place within. It is a life changing experience. Participating in a sacred journey may introduce us and open us up to many things we may not have known about before, including the equinoxes, solstices, full moons, the five initiations of Christ, Mary Magdalene and the grail mysteries, water initiations, labyrinths, the magic and mystery of Lourdes, ancient wisdom, Avatars of light, beings and entities of light, masters and saints, healing energies and the eight gateways of the year which we enter through, and much more. Each country's sacred sites open us to new awarenesses through their particular matrix and configuration. They are living temples, museums. As one experiences sacred sites, temples, pyramids, monasteries, churches, mounds, round towers and other monuments and formations; one gets the feeling that something really mystical and magical has happened here in the past and in some places is still happening in the present as they are all places, vortexes of light consciousness connected with, and to, higher vibrations. We have amazing Atlantian temples (remnants from the continent of Atlantis) in Ireland, Malta, Egypt and many other places that were used in ancient times to capture the energies of the Cosmos. Each one of these sacred places is dedicated to a certain purpose. Newgrange, in Ireland, for instance, is a Goddess Temple whose main purpose was to generate light. It was all about rejuvenation, fertility and rebirth. We have Glendalough Monastery in County Wicklow, in Ireland. Its mystical entrance is built in perfect balance indicating a place of the unified consciousness of the Divine Feminine connected to all of the elemental kingdoms, the realm of fairies, devas and such. A visit here is a life changing experience. There are so many inter-dimensional experiences to be had on the ancient sites from Iona in Scotland, to Lake Titicaca partly in Peru and partly in Bolivia; to Tara in Ireland, and the Pyramids in Egypt at Giza. Each site and country offers a particular experience of awakening and shifting of consciousness in its own way. You could have spiritual experiences in Ireland where you may connect with the druids, or the goddess, Saint Brigid with her druidic flame that burned for over one thousand years until Cromwell had it extinguished. You may learn about how, and when, the Pope brought about "Peters Pence", a taxation of Irish households in twelfth century. In France you may connect with the energy of Mary Magdalene, the Grail Family, Mother Mary, Saint Sarah, the Black Madonna's, the Knights Templar and the Cathars. Traveling to sites in France is an amazing transformational and healing journey. It is truly a journey of deeper awakening as it connects on all levels with the beauty and symbolism stored in its sacred places connecting to the Divine Feminine within each of us. It awakens each of us to Mary Magdalene and the importance of unified consciousness. And so it goes, with each sacred journey, and each country. The sacred sites call us. Sometimes we are not sure why we are taking this journey, we only know that it is calling us. We just know we have to go on a particular tour, for some reason. All is eventually revealed as we journey and have our, ah ha moments giving us the understanding of its holy purpose somewhere along the way. People can have amazing experiences on a sacred site journey. I will share with you a few examples of experiences I've had.

In Ireland my guide is usually Mother Mary. She is my perpetual light and has been since my first experience with her in May 1990. When I go on a tour, I have no idea who will show up as my guide from the other side. On a recent tour to Egypt, I was surprised when Vera Stanley Alder showed up. She was an English Mystic born in 1898 who passed away in 1984. She wrote many spiritual books in the nineteen thirties. The first book of hers I read was, "Finding the Third Eye". The first day I arrived in Cairo she appeared and told me she was going to be my guide in Egypt. Each morning she would give me a message. Then she told me what to bring and what I would need for the ceremony that day. She would also let me know if I was forgetting something I would need that day as I was walking out my hotel or bedroom door. In Italy my most profound experiences were at the Basilica of Saint Frances of Assisi. At his tomb I went into a deep meditation. My participants on this sacred site tour said they felt an amazing rush of energy while I was meditating there, which lasted about five minutes. Next I took them to the side altar of Saint Anthony. Here again, a huge vibrational shift took place, according to the people traveling with me. They were pushed back about eight feet from me as

my arms gradually moved up above my head, of their own accord, creating the shape of a chalice in which powerful energy flowed down through me and out to others. The next altar we visited was just a few feet away. It was the Altar of Mary Magdalene. Here, like at the others altars and tomb, the energy started to flow. My hands again moved up above my head and the energy continued to flow, pushing people back even further. They believed a vortex was being opened. A lady by the name of Christine Barnes did a drawing of me, as this was happening.

I was also informed by the group that the two priests who were hearing confession, when this process started, stopped hearing confession after my first experience and just came in close and watched me as I went through these experiences. At the end of all of this, I needed to sit down and rest. These experiences still happen to me each time I visit Assisi. The other place in Italy I have had major experiences is at the Basilica di Santa Maria Maggiore. Within this basilica is an amazing Black Madonna. Here again, I've have had many experiences where I was taken to my knees. In this one experience the energy was so intense I was first taken down to my knees and then all the way down to the floor ending up lying face down, prostrate on the floor, holding my arms out as the gift of a baby (Jesus) was put in my arms by Mother Mary. All of this happened while I was in an expanded, altered state of semi-consciousness. In Peru, I've had Lord Melchizedek leading me through our journey in a similar way to when Vera Stanley Alder guided me, each day, in Egypt. Lord Melchizedek leading our journey through Peru, culminated in an amazing ritual on Lake Titicaca. Each person in the group had profound experiences as they felt a major shift take place within themselves on this crystalline lake of Illumination. In Bolivia, our unseen guide was Master Saint Germain. And so it goes with each tour, I just allow, accept and follow the guidance which shows up. Going to the Casa of Saint Ignatius of Loyola (John of God's compound) is more of a sacred pilgrimage than a sacred journey. Spending time at the Casa is an amazing spiritual pilgrimage as it offers powerful energies within a crystalline portal in Abadiania, Brazil. Even though John of God is no longer physically there, the energies are still there. It is an extremely powerful, spiritually rich, and deeply transformative place for experiences on all levels of body, mind and spirit. The Casa is a home away from home with its uniqueness of familiarity and its welcoming, supportive environment for deepening processes of purification, healing and connections on all levels. This process is one that changes not only the energetic potential of all physical and energetic bodies within one's being, but also elevates and invites changes to occur through positive manifestations and new creations in one's life. This happens through connection with the entities and beings of light, healing and love which are present here. The environment is majestic at the Casa. Beautiful people at the Casa open their arms and hearts to welcome and assist all, which is what allows miracles to occur in ways that are energetically seen and felt. It is because of the collective group consciousness formed by the global community present in this physical space at any one moment in time, that the immense capacity for healing on all levels takes place. Whether you are looking for relief in the spiritual, physical, mental or emotional body; or you are just coming here for your deeper spiritual journey in connection and re-treating in spirit, this sacred pilgrimage will impact your life in such profound ways, you will not ever be the same again. Here you will find a deeper connection within your own spirit… no matter what one's intention upon arrival, tremendous benefits and expansions will be gifts to your body, mind and spirit for you to take home.

In February 2005, I was on my way to Gallup, New Mexico from Tucson to visit a friend in the hospital there who was about to make his transition. I was on route, driving through Winslow, Arizona one early morning, when Mother Mary appeared in the back seat of my car and asked, "Is it not time you started doing

Divine Feminine Conferences?" I responded, "I will look into it when I get home." Normally I would have said or asked something else but this time I just accepted it without question as it felt so right. I had come to understand when Mother Mary came to me in my car, as I drove, I did not question anymore. I knew all would be in divine order. If I had additional questions, I could ask later. So it was that the first Divine Feminine Conference came about in May 2005 in Tucson. We had incredible presenters, including Margaret Starbird (author of The Woman with the Alabaster Jar), Flo Magdalena (author of I Remember Union: The Story of Mary Magdalena) and Claire Heartsong (author of Anna, Grandmother of Jesus). Other speakers followed in 2006 when the conference was offered in Phoenix, Dublin and in Reading in the United Kingdom. This was an amazing expansive time for me as I had to stand up in front of people and present a ninety minute talk on the Divine Feminine, which was particularly challenging as I had not done any public speaking up to this point. Also there were some people who firmly believed that men knew nothing about the Divine Feminine. In 2007, I offered a Divine Feminine conference in Tucson, Arizona and New York. In October of that year I once again arranged a Divine Feminine conference in Dublin and one in London. I also arranged a mini four-day tour in between these two locations traveling to the Isle of Iona and elsewhere in Scotland with eight other people involved with the conference. This is when the events I've written about in the introduction occurred and changed my life forever.

23

THE NATURE DOCTOR/
MATRIX NUTRIENTS

s a result of the time I spent in Muskogee, I suffered two serious ailments. Soon after being incarcerated I started to develop soft lumps under my skin. I wondered what these things were and what was happening to my body. It seemed that I was suffering from malnutrition. The jail doctor decided I needed more greens and ordered a double helping of vegetables for me; but everything was canned which didn't do much good. My body had another problem to deal with as well; during my stay there I also developed severe arthritis in my back. The prison cells were very cold and were kept that way to discourage bacteria from growing. In addition, I only had two thin blankets and slept on a very thin foam mattress on top of a steel frame that held the cold fiercely. My body didn't have a chance. Many a time I cried with arthritic pain. I tried on many occasions to get another mattress to absorb the cold from the steel frame which was embedded into the exterior wall of the cell, to no avail. After being released from prison, this continued over the years as I guided the tours. In 2003, when I moved to Arizona, I spent most of the winter months in Tucson where I was based. The warm climate helped me somewhat, but the pain persisted. I had tried everything and done lots of research on many products and their effects on the body. Finally the solution presented itself in 2008. I was at the Crop Circle Conference in Marlborough, England, and John, a friend of mine said, "Finbarr, I have found a product that helps arthritis." He introduced me to Silica and Silica gel. By that time I had already spent many years studying vitamins and supplements and anything else that would alleviate my problems, but I found out most of the supplements were from man-made chemicals. I refused to use them. This Silica was organic, all natural, and made from micro-organisms in sand! It absolutely worked for me. The arthritic pain left. I found my joints were much more nimble because the Silica lubricated my joints. Not only did it lubricate my joints, but it also helped my hair and nails to grow. My body loved this product. I knew I could help a lot of other people with similar ailments as well. John put me in touch with the manufacturer in Spain. So it was that in November 2008, I received my first shipment of Silica. As I used the product, I realized that the vibration of the silica also affected my crystalline body; it affected my physical and etheric body, as well as affecting me on a cellular level. In fact, it came to me that the silica was one of the most important products for anyone traveling the ascension path. Somehow something in it facilitates that body's ascent on the pathway of the heart. Once I realized this, I knew that in order for us humans to fully engage and benefit from the new energies and the gateways, our bodies had to be prepared to hold the higher vibrations. I now knew what I had to do. I knew I needed to develop a line of supplements of the highest quality and vibration that could be incorporated along with the Divine Feminine Emotional Healing work to help people with their healing and ascension process. I could offer a complete package for their health and well-being. I was very excited. I just had to find the right ingredients and the right formulas. The Universe was now encouraging me to take my next step. Immediately after I had dealt with my arthritis, Spirit told me I was done in the desert. It was now time to move to the mountains. So I packed my belongings and moved to Colorado Springs, the home of the Christian right, the Air Force academy and Fort Carson. I wondered, what am I doing in this ultra-conservative town? There was an undercurrent of 'us versus them' being fought out in many ways particularly in the school board elections. After four years, Spirit shifted me first southwest to Durango, Colorado where I stayed for two years, and then Mother Mary pointed me in the direction of Montrose, Colorado. I continued my quest to find a bio-chemist who would help me produce a line of vitamins and supplements that were pure, free from wheat, starch, gluten, soy, added sugars, colourings, flavourings and preservatives. I wanted them manufactured with filtered water only, suitable for everyone, including vegetarians and vegans. In March 2009, I was in New York at an Integrative Health Expo where I started chatting to a nearby lady. As we talked, I told her what I was looking for. She knew exactly who I needed to connect with and she gave me his contact information. On Saturday morning when I returned home, I emailed him. Within twenty minutes I received a phone call from the man, Eric Llewellyn. It turned out he was, in fact, an amazing alchemist in his own right! Shortly thereafter we met. It felt like we were even more than old buddies, it was like we were old soul-mates. There was something about his energy that was so familiar. So it was that The Nature Doctor line of vitamins and supplements was born. I had a vision of what I wanted these products to embody. I wanted products to make us strong so we could walk the pathway of ascension and hold a higher level of vibration. I knew how hard it was for me to focus on spirituality and the ascension process when I was tired, or in pain. So I wanted to design inspired vitamins and supplements with this in mind. I knew that for me, and other light workers, to be able to continue doing our work we needed products that would, in fact, support this. I wanted them to hold a high vibrational frequency which would help heal the physical and emotional body, while also helping the etheric body. The great thing was, I did not need to explain any of this to Eric. He understood this was a sacred undertaking. Instead of me trying to give him the understanding, the Universe had already given it to both him and me. By the time of our third meeting I knew why the energy around Eric was familiar, so I asked him, "What is your connection with Master Saint Germain?" He was surprised! "How do you know about that?" To which I answered, "I just know." That took our relationship to a whole new level as he knew exactly where I was coming from. We knew these vitamins and supplements were divinely inspired. From there, we as the alchemist and his fellow traveller, worked with a new deeper understanding of our undertaking. We created formulas and developed protocols that helped with Cancer, Diabetes, Candida, Gluten, Fibromyalgia, sugar cravings and many other targeted issues. We also focused on designing products which would help support the body's own immune system so it could better assist the body's natural process of fighting against various cancers, including cancer of the oesophagus, breast cancer, liver cancer, colon cancer and prostate cancer. We shopped around until we found a supplier of blue glass bottles which we knew could hold, and would not dissipate, the vibration of our products. Needless to say, as a result of all of this, my body is now strong and solid. The Nature Doctor is my pride and joy. I will be forever grateful to Mother Mary and Divine Mother for allowing me to be part of this. I changed the name to Matrix Nutrients in 2015 so it would be more in keeping with what is was offering. Matrix Nutrients are, quite simply, food without the bulk. Our vitamins and minerals are truly natural supplements, made using high quality ingredients, in a whole food matrix. They can provide your body with the levels of nutrients our ancestors consumed, as nature intended. Because they are made from real food, your body is able to absorb and use the active nutrients much more efficiently. In contrast to other so-called 'natural' supplements, since ours are made from foods, not chemicals, the body recognizes these supplements as foods which are absorbed within the blood stream within twenty minutes of taking them. Their rate of absorption is at minimum, 85%. Due to their high bio-availability status, and hence the low potency requirements, there are no known side effects to Whole Food Matrix Nutrients. The use of yeast during the mineral growth process, means "Whole Food" products are also non-allergenic. The unique "growth" process of Matrix Nutrients results in delivery systems of nutrients that ensure high bioavailability of effective doses of the desired nutrients to appropriate sites within the body where it is needed most. My work now is focused on my sacred tours, the shift, ascension and the new dispensation along with the work of the Golden Flame in conjunction with my supplements, Matrix Nutrients. I do this because my passion and my desire, is to assist others who are going through the Ascension Process which is the pathway to Self-Realization, Unified Consciousness/Christ Consciousness. Our ultimate mission as a collective and individual consciousness is to arrive at a place of Unified Consciousness and Oneness, to let go of fear and duality and allow ourselves to be led by Spirit. I believe I can assist in this. I believe, just like I did in Northern Ireland, that there is a Higher Justice, a Divine Plan, and that we are all being divinely guided. My part is to do my best each day to walk in harmony with that Divine Plan and follow the Pathway of the Heart.

24

MY PERSONAL JOURNEY IN THE ESSENE AND CATHAR INITIATION CAVES

In 2012, I was in France where I had some amazing experiences. For some years I had been thinking that I should explore Mount Bugarach where the ancient Essenes, the Jewish sect that Jesus came from, had a community as I was there in June with an opportunity to be in the area for a week so. Through my friend, Eugene, I found a guide, Harvey, to take me on an expedition to visit the Cathedral Cave and anything else that he was willing to show me. On the morning we met he said to me "So you want to visit the Cathedral Cave? And what else do you want to see and experience?" I asked "What is there for me to experience?" Harvey asks me "Are you open to going into a cave for an Essene Initiation?" and I say "Yes," and we set off for Mt. Bugarach with our translator Tim. Upon arrival we start to climb for about 45 minutes. Just ahead of us we could see an opening to a cave. Before reaching the entrance, Harvey stopped and pointed out a black snake to me. It was about 4 feet long and it looked very peaceful. After admiring the snake and watching it climb out on a branch we proceeded to the cave. Then Harvey asks me to take all the metal off my body, my watch, etc. as we are going to be entering this cave in the dark. He asked me if I was OK with that. I said yes, not fully understanding what I was letting myself in for. He hands me a headband with a light on it to put around my head, but tells me we will not be putting on the light until we get all the way inside the cave, which is about 150 yards. Next he gets down on his knees and starts to crawl in through a hole in the cave which is about 30 inches in diameter. Tim tells me to follow him. Now, I have to tell you, I was not prepared for this, so I got down on all fours and proceed to follow him through the hole. Tim assures me he will be right behind me and for me to just follow Harvey. Off we go, but about 12 feet in I get claustrophobic and say I have got to get out. I start to back out and hit my head on a rock and get two gashes. Harvey, through Tim, tells me I am perfectly safe that he is in front of me, Tim is behind me and I need to breathe. He says, when I go into fear, I ask for a symbol to enter my head and he told me to continue to look at this symbol in my imagination until my breathing is under control again. I closed my eyes searching for a symbol. The symbol I got was a snake, so off we set again and this time I was much calmer. We continued in the tunnel, through the dark, on all fours, which was not easy as the pebbles on the cave floor were not too kind to one's knees. I was moving along nicely until I felt that I was going down an incline. I stopped and started to panic. I used my symbol to get my breathing back to and even level. Tim asks me what was wrong. I told him it feels like there is a big drop in the floor ahead of me and yes, indeed, there was. Tim spoke with Harvey and discovered that Harvey forgot to mention that in this section I needed to go feet first and then back to all fours as there was about a three foot drop. Looking back on this later I realized this whole adventure was symbolic of the birthing tunnel, being reborn. Finally I got to a place where Harvey asks me to stand up. We are still in the dark. After about ten minutes of quiet meditation, he asks me to turn my light on, which I did. I found myself in a massive cave with what looked like a lake in it. Harvey asked me to take off my shoes and socks and roll up my pants as were now going to walk through this water which was about ten to twelve inches deep and continued on around a corner through some rocks. I followed Harvey through the water and boy was it cold! But after going about 30 feet it no longer felt cold, so I continued on for at least another 100 feet. Then we were in another large cave which was beautiful. As I stepped out of the water onto a dry rock, I had an amazing experience where in an expanded, altered, state of consciousness, I was greeted by several beings. One of these beings was Joseph of Arimathea. He did all the talking. He informed me I had just completed a major divine Essene Initiation. I became aware of many beings of Light surrounding me; Mother Mary, Mary Magdalene, Master Jesus, Master St. Germain, Hilarion, El Morya and other Beings of Light whom I did not know by name. It was an amazing, mystical and magical experience which lasted quite a long time. All during this time, Harvey and Tim just stood and watched me have my experience. It was so magical I was vibrating at an amazing rate with lots of energy coursing through my body. After some time Harvey asked me if I was ready to go back out. I said yes. Then he tells me I am to go back out, on my own, with the light on. He and Tim would follow me shortly. But this was something I had to do on my own so I could fully understand all that had happened. It took me some time to get out as I had to go back through the water and then put my shoes and socks back on so I could proceed back out through the tunnel. It gave me some time to process everything. I worked my way out to the cave entrance. I was amazed at all that had transpired over the course of the morning. Shortly, thereafter, Harvey and Tim arrived and we made our way back down the mountain in silence. Then we had a break to have our picnic lunch. After lunch we got back in Harvey's car and drove to the other side of Mount Bugarach where we again started to climb, which we did for over an hour. Finally, we reached the Cathedral Cave, which was a massive cave. This was just an amazing experience! What a wonderful cave this was, with so much energy. But I have to say, it was nothing to match the experience at the initiation cave. On the day I met Harvey and Tim, Harvey also asked me if I want to have a Cathar experience as well as an Essene experience. (The Cathars were a Gnostic group which flourished particularly in the Languedoc Region of France in the 11th and 12th centuries. They regarded men and women as equal. They lived ethically believing there was no separation between them and God.) Of course I said yes! He told me about a Cathar initiation cave. At 8 am the following morning I met Tim and we drove in my car to meet Harvey, who lived on the way to the Cathar caves. It took us about an hour to drive there. We stopped on the way to pick up a picnic lunch and get some tea and coffee. Harvey first took me to the cave of the two churches. One was much larger than the other. It was absolutely huge and had light streaming in through the roof in one corner. We explored this cave for about an hour and came to a point where it was sealed off. Harvey told me that the government had sealed it off to protect a large amount of wall paintings within the cave until they found a way to let people view them while also protecting them from vandalism. We next explored the sister cave of the two churches which was much smaller but had a very sacred energy. It was obvious that lots of rituals had been performed in this sacred place, whereas the larger cave felt like it was the place where the Cathars might have lived. We climbed back down to the road and drove further along so that we could again start climbing up to the Cathar Initiation Cave. Upon reaching this cave, Harvey tells me "Finbarr we are going to do the same thing as yesterday. We will enter the cave in the dark on all fours, but first we will have to walk some distance through the cave in the dark until we get to the entrance to the tunnel." I say OK. He says just follow my voice. So I follow his voice on foot for about a 50 yards. Then he tells me to get down on all fours and follow him, follow his voice. I ask how far in I had to go on all fours and he says a little longer than yesterday. Harvey was a man of few words. He allowed you to have an experience and then he would discuss it with you. But getting any information from him about it, beforehand was not easy, it was all about trust. So off we set on all fours. I felt much calmer than yesterday so I was in a good place. After a while, Harvey asked me to stand up. When I did, I had an experience again, in an altered state of consciousness, with a being (Mother Mary) which lasted for about ten minutes. Then Harvey asked me if I was ready to move on, so off we went again, me following his voice with Tim bringing up the rear. We would take another break where, again, Harvey asked me to stand up. When I did, I had another experience with another being (Mary Magdalene). This process went on for some time. Finally Harvey asked me to switch on my light where I then saw we were in the most magnificent cave. I then asked him how many stops we had made. I was in an extremely altered state having had experiences on the way into the cave with many different beings. He said "Seven Finbarr, one for each chakra." Now I understood why he would not tell me anything before we started. He wanted me to have my experience at each stop with the beings, the different masters that appeared. This cave was both a little easier and somewhat harder than the Essene cave in that the floor was smoother, but some of the openings in the tunnels were not as large. We were literally crawling on our bellies, on a few occasion, to get through an opening as we explored the cave in all of its mysticism. We became aware of some amazing symbols which had formed over thousands of years as drops of water fell from the roof of the cave creating pillars. One was a beautiful Goddess. One was of a triple Goddess with a phallic symbol next to it, and then a castle. We spent a very long time in this cave as the energy and the formations were truly extraordinary. When you walked, you had to look at your feet to make sure they were on the ground because you felt like you were floating. Finally as I followed Harvey, we worked our way back out through all the areas of the seven chakra experiences this time with our lights on as there

197

were many tunnels and offshoots where it could have been easy to get lost. Again, this was another life-altering experience.

When we got outside Harvey now told me we need to go to the Bethlehem Cave and he asked me if I was up for that. The Cathar Initiations were always completed at the Bethlehem Cave, as it was a place of thanksgiving and rebirth, so off we travelled to the cave. Upon reaching it, one could only know they were in a very special place. Upon entering it, I was immediately drawn to an amazing rock that was about eight feet in diameter. I walked over and asked for permission to lie on it. Harvey tells me that lying on that rock, or altar, was part of the Cathar initiation. While I was on the altar, Harvey climbed the wall to a height about 4 feet above the floor and put himself on the wall in a cruciform position. He stayed up there and then he said to me, after I finished on the altar, "Do you want to put yourself on the wall?" This you could do by using the toes of your shoes on tiny stones sticking out of the wall. The trick he said was to turn yourself around so your back is to the wall enabling you to stretch your arms out. You had to balance your body on one leg (toe) so as to swing your body around in order to get positioned to put yourself against the wall with your arms outstretched. This was an incredible experience. When I got down off the wall, and walked around the cave a few times, Harvey asked me if I was ready for the final part of the initiation. Of course I was! I found myself standing in the centre of the cave with its wide open expanse, looking across the valley to another mountain. I now wondered what he wanted me to do next. He told me I needed to go through the re-birthing process. He then took me up to the end of the cave where there is a large opening with about a 500 foot drop. To the right of the opening is a small hole in the rock, about two feet in diameter. He then tells me I will need to crawl through the hole with great care because the ledge is very small. I would also need to enter the cave through the large opening, being mindful of the 500 foot drop. What he did not tell me was that as I went through this opening, I was going to have a major experience of being re-birthed energetically. As I put my head and upper body though the opening I felt I was in another dimension. My head and upper body felt light and wonderful while the lower part of my body, still inside the cave, felt very heavy. This process continued until my whole body was through the channel. Then I felt completely light and I walked back in through the large opening of the cave feeling totally renewed and refreshed. That day brought to a close my experience with the Essenes and Cathars on this trip.

25

THE FIVE YEARS OF
TRANSPARENCY AND THE
GATEWAYS

As I mentioned in my Introduction, I was in a little side alcove in Iona Abbey when I was given the message: "You are here because you agreed to be here at this time to bring forth the new dispensation, which will start at the Winter Solstice. The world will enter a five-year period of transparency with a different focus, each year, but with the underlying energy being transparency." I shared the message with my group, some of whom, were presenters at the conference. They accepted what I said, but I told them I was seeking confirmation of this message. As I have already shared, I asked for confirmation. Two days later I received it in Rosslyn Chapel. To refresh your memory of this story, I was showing a member of the group an energy vortex and was then sauntering to another energy spot when I was approached by a lady who said, "My name is Judy. I am from Atlanta, Georgia. Spirit has asked me to give you a message." Then she said, "This is all very strange. I have never done anything like this before. Are you open to receiving a message?" I nodded and said yes and she then gave me the same message I had received on Iona. This was my confirmation. In the meantime, the group gathered around me and we looked at each other wondering what this meant for each of us. That winter of 2007, I found myself celebrating the Winter Solstice in Tucson, Arizona. As part of this celebration, we ushered in the period of Transparency. A couple of weeks later when 2008 arrived, it was quickly apparent the year would embody transparency; in oneself, in government and in businesses. There was no place to hide as the whistle-blowers came forward. Much was revealed and many changes occurred. It also became apparent that what was happening on a global level was also happening on an individual level as well. I heard many stories of friends and strangers being asked to look deep within themselves and to make changes. It was a year of inner work. It was a year of looking at oneself with new eyes, seeing the things we've been brushing under the carpet in hope they would just go away so we would not have to look at them. But now, with the new energies of transparency, this practice of hiding everything under the rug was no longer possible on an individual, family, corporate or government level. All issues, both personal and global, all the places where actions have been without integrity, started to come out into the open to be dealt with now, or if not we would have to deal with the consequences. Winter Solstice 2008 came and I asked for us to contemplate compassion as we entered 2009. We were asked to feel this in our own life, as well as for the people in government and business who had been exposed, and accused, of wrongdoing by the whistle-blowers. We were also asked to feel that same compassion for ourselves. It is sometimes very hard to feel compassion for oneself, but at this time it was crucial. Part of understanding compassion involves learning to be non-judgemental, simply being able to be an observer, using discernment and detachment, allowing the process to emerge.

On 9/9/9 I was in Southern France leading a group tour to experience the energies of Mary Magdalene, which at this time, was a magical and transformational journey for the group on all levels. Compassion for ourselves and for the world around us, was the theme for the journey. Mary Magdalene takes no prisoners, you are there to receive a divine initiation. She brings the energies of the issues, one needs to look at right up in front of your face. Being in her frequency expands the awareness of the issue so you can find its resolution. It is up to you how you respond. These are always life-changing moments. Anything to do with Mary Magdalene is life changing. Although she takes no prisoners, she also gives a very clear message. Although she is tough, she, of course, is very compassionate in the giving of her messages. She expects you to follow through, however tough it may be. The Winter Solstice of 2009 radiated Balance and so the next year 2010, was about finding the power within ourselves that equilibrium brings. That very much involved honouring and developing a balance of the male and female within us; expressing and acknowledging the sacred union unified consciousness, and the respect for oneself and others. It entails standing in our own power, listening to our bodies and the messages from within. Our power/balance also emanates from our body temple as we become aware of what we ingest, paying attention to our food and reading labels so as to become more aware of what we eat, as well as what we ingest as environmental and electronic influences. We can also find balance in the power of our voice through becoming more aware of what we say or chant, by learning to be impeccable with our words because the sounds and vibrations we emit are commands to the universe thus creating our reality. Our voice and how we choose to use it, is of major importance as we quest life's pathway.

On 10/10/10, I was in Egypt with a group to experience the ancient wisdom inhabited there particularly as we experienced private time at the great Pyramid at Giza and at the Sphinx. We knew we were at one of the three major connection points in the world focused on bringing forth the new consciousness; the other two being Tara in Ireland and Lake Titicaca in Peru. We cruised the Nile River experiencing the ancient temples at Aswan, Luxor and many more places in this land of ancient wisdom with all its mystery. As we travelled here, we also honoured the sacred union we found within ourselves bringing us balance and power in our lives. Traveling to these sites in Egypt raised our vibrations, bringing each of us to a place of greater wisdom, opening us up to the power of love and illumination as we found that same balance and power within us as we quested the mysteries and initiations. Winter Solstice 2010 offered us Resurrection as the theme of 2011, it offered an opportunity to resurrect our inner selves and to connect with our divine spirit on all levels. It provided the space for us to look at our lives so that we could reclaim our power and our innate ability to manifest and create new forms. Part of this Resurrection was to let go of all that no longer served us in our lives. It also brought forth the Arab Spring, a series of anti-government protests, uprisings, and armed rebellions which spread across North Africa and the Middle East bringing about many changes in Egypt and the Middle East. With the people of Egypt reclaiming their power and taking their rightful place in the world and in the Middle East, people worked to release the shackles of the past and to reclaim their power!

On 11/11/11, I was in Peru with a group at the Gate of the Gods or Doorway of Lord Amamu Muru (purported to be a Master who escaped from Lemuria). We worked with the energies of this magical place to open a doorway within our own hearts. The process was enabling us to cross the threshold, awakening us to the universal consciousness and further opening us up to the second coming of Christ which is taking place within each of us. The stage had been set for us to receive this initiation because we spent the day before on the crystalline lake, Lake Titicaca. This amazingly powerful crystalline lake is also connected to ancient Atlantis and is aligned, as I mentioned before, to Tara in Ireland and to the great Pyramid at Giza through a major ley line which runs from Lake Titicaca to the Great Pyramid. 11/11/11 was a time of great awakening of resurrection and divine initiations within each of us and of course, within all of humanity. Winter Solstice 2011 brought us the issue of Ascension for 2012. In preparing us for 2012, shifting vibrations/energies came forth to help us release all that was no longer in alignment in our evolving lives. It brought plenty of divorces, both in marriages and in business and other partnerships. Friends also disappeared from our lives, if those friendships no longer served our higher purpose. All of these people and situations fell away so we could reclaim our true selves and new friends arrived. We continued to evolve and embraced the new vibrations that surrounded us, after all we are vibrational beings! We became more consciously aware of who we really are, and of our "I AM" presence.

On 12/12/12 I was with a group in Guatemala. Here we connected with the ancient Mayan culture as we engaged in three sacred ceremonies. These ceremonies included a water ceremony on Lake Atilan and a Mayan ceremony of gratitude on the sacred mountain known as Cerro Del Oro (mountain of gold). This is an ancient Mayan ceremonial site facilitated by the High Oracle of the Maya. Another very special ceremony took place at the La Laguna Sacred Mayan ceremonial site. These sacred ceremonies were a major transformational time for all concerned as we experienced the cleansing of the sacred crystalline water, climbed Cerro Del Oro, and worked with sacred fire at these ceremonial sites. Here we had our final opportunities to release all that no longer, collectively, served us. It was a major moment in shifting the energies and the vibration of our planet and all who dwell upon it. We have been looking at all of these energy shifts and transformations taking place during the Winter Solstices on the planet, but what started this cycle called the New Age, was the Harmonic Convergence. This marked the ending of time as we have known it, and the birth of a new time cycle. Every twenty six thousand years the universe makes a shift and that is what Harmonic Convergence was all about in August of 1987. At that time, our spiritual maturity was measured as the Avatars of Light, The Great White Brotherhood, assessed our planet to see if we were ready to move forward spiritually or if we would go deeper into decline. It was decided we were ready to move forward. With the decision made to move forward, we then moved into a new construction phase so that the magnetic grid changes which started at the Harmonic Convergence would be completed by Winter Solstice 2012. We are now in the beginning times of a New Earth as the crystalline grids are opening up making accessible its stored information and ancient wisdom. We are being asked to connect more deeply with the consciousness of nature and the earth so our lives will be completely supported as we move forward in understanding, and co-creating, the New Earth. As part of this shift, we are now experiencing planetary changes, changes within humanity, and changes within ourselves as we absorb the new energies and the new consciousness. The crystalline children born at the end of the last century are leading the way. They are now being joined by the Millennium children, children born since January 1st 2000. These children are creating the shift because they are wired differently; their DNA is more evolved and they are creating an upward shift in consciousness. We ourselves, are being asked, each day, to be aware of the up-shift in our life and consciousness taking place within ourselves as we let go of habits and verbiage which no longer serves us and holds in it negativity. As negative words and phrases such as; try, have to, never, should, good, and bad are eliminated from our vocabulary, vibrationally we then move up to another level. We all know that if we make a statement like, "I would never do that again" the universe will test us by sending us a challenge to see if we would do that again or not. We are now in a time when the new energies of the fifth dimension are bleeding in through the Seven Rays, seven streams

206

of energy from the Great Central Sun, which are being filtered to earth through the Big Dipper. So it is for each of us to be aware of the new energies we are interfacing with as we have shifting DNA as we move towards crystalline consciousness. GMO food are not in alignment with our new body vibrations as we each emit a vibration, an energy, and a frequency. We are being asked to listen to our bodies and feel what we need and what is now right for us. If we ask our bodies and listen, we will get an answer. If fear controls us, we cannot expand as fear is an illusion. We are used to being controlled by the Church, by the State, and by religion through fear. Now, it is our government who is working against us, to control us through fear. It is time to stand up and say no more. We have had enough control through fear. Our millennium children will not tolerate oppressive governments seeking to control our lives and our money. I state, I am claiming my independence. It is for each of us to strive, each day, to reclaim our independence (not just on Independence Day). It is time to lift ourselves out from under the control of the unholy trinity of the United States, United Kingdom and Israel with their creeping fascist agenda which every day takes away people's rights and freedoms. Everywhere in the world that you find chaos, you will find the unholy trinity behind it. The constitution was shredded during the Bush/Chaney/Obama years and our millennial children will claim it back. If fear controls us we cannot expand. Fear is an invitation inviting us to expand our power and our curiosity and as we do so we delve within and explore this fear by turning it into curiosity which is an amazing life changing experience because once you explore and recognize it you find there is nothing to fear. It is only when we allow light to shine in our lives that we will burn through it. Life is a vibrational journey of awareness, healing and transformation. As we embrace each challenge in our life, with love and light, we know that as we do indeed embrace each challenge, we will grow in deeper understanding of our divine self and our life. When we are in alignment with our spiritual nature, we take the steps that help us on the pathway of ascension. Our higher self has memory of all our lifetimes. Our higher self becomes us when we come to fully understand that God is within us and we are connected to all of creation. We come to understand that unity is in all things, because how I treat you, reflects on me and my vibration. We are part of the collective Oneness. As we move forward we come to understand our Avatar consciousness, our Unity Consciousness, our Unified or Christ Consciousness. Ascension happens through vibrational, energetic and consciousness shifts. It has taken us two thousand years of gestation to reach this point, since the Christ Consciousness or Unified Consciousness, was birthed upon earth at the time of the crucifixion. The old ways are falling away. As in any birth/death process, it can be painful. Chaos may reign, but ultimately all will be well as we breathe new life. Now is the time of the 'second coming'. This is what is happening within each one of us as we understand we are spiritual beings, having a spiritual experience. It is for each of us to understand that there is no such person as Jesus Christ, also known as Jesus of Nazareth. There is no Mr Christ. Jesus was a man and Christ is the consciousness which Jesus brought to ground on earth. Mary Magdalene is the soul of that consciousness; Jesus sowed the seed and she birthed it. This consciousness has been abused for the past two thousand years by various religions who did not teach or practice the message that Jesus brought. It was used to control through fear and judgment. We are now at the time of a new birth, the second coming, and the spiritual birth. This is taking place within each of us as the energy of the golden flame, a spiritual energy that burns within each of us, the flame of love without reservation which vibrates within our hearts, emanates out into the world. Remember there is no such person as Mr Christ. There is only Unity, Unified or Christ Consciousness which every being on this planet is imbued with. With this awareness we become a witness without judgment, detached in a way we each understand. We can stand outside the box and view the situation without emotion. We awaken the power and awareness within ourselves so that when we send energy to a situation, we know it will go to where it is most needed. The age of the crystalline energy of creation which we are now living in, comes with information and gifts of spirit that serves us on all levels. Ascension happens through sacred vibrational and energetic shifts; every 45 days we are in a planetary vibrational shift. This can be explained through the sacred journey/geography of the sun with its Eight Cycles of the Wheel of the year. These create sacred vibrational and energetic shifts on the planet and within each of us. This yearly wheel has 4 major spokes and 4 minor spokes which supports the planet. The Winter Solstice, a major spoke, usually on December 21st, is the beginning of each year's cycle. The second minor spoke is February 1st. Next is a major spoke, the Spring Equinox on March 21st which is the time of perfect balance. The Fourth minor spoke is May 1st. The next

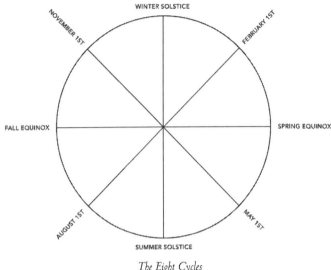

The Eight Cycles

major spoke is the Summer Solstice on June 21st, the year's highest peak point of vibrational energy. The sixth minor spoke is August 1st. Next is a major spoke, the Autumn Equinox on September 21st, a time of perfect balance. Finally this is followed by a minor spoke, the 8th and final spoke of the year, November 1st taking us back to Winter Solstice so the cycle can begin again with a new energy and vibration. Dates shift by a day or two depending on the zodiac calendar. Each of the four seasons is also governed by a planetary archangel. The Winter Solstice is governed by Archangel Gabriel who brings Love. The Spring Equinox is Archangel Raphael bringing Healing. The Summer Solstice, Archangel Uriel, bringing Beauty and the Autumn Equinox, Archangel Michael, who brings Purification. As we awaken to the new dispensation, going within and embracing the new dawn, there are certain affirmations, prayers, mantras and meditations to help oneself and humanity in moving forward. The World Healing Meditation, the first one listed below, is normally said around the world at Noon on New Year's Eve. It is a very powerful meditation to practice each day however, if you so wish. Other prayers and invocations have been included which help us to remember who we are and to awaken to the new dispensation. Suggestions of prayers to use for embracing the new dawn are also listed below:

THE WORLD HEALING MEDITATION
In the beginning ... In the beginning God.
In the beginning God created the heaven and the earth.
And God said, "Let there be light!"
And there was light.
Now is the time of the new beginning.
I am a co–creator with God, and it is a new Heaven that comes as the Good Will of God is expressed on Earth through me.
It is the Kingdom of Light, Love, Peace and Understanding.
And I am doing my part to reveal its Reality.
I begin with me.
I am a living Soul and the Spirit of God dwells in me, as me.
I and the Father are one, and all that the Father has is mine.
IN TRUTH I, I AM THE CHRIST OF GOD
What is true of me is true of everyone, for God is all and all is God.
I see only the Spirit of God in every Soul.
And to every man, woman and child on Earth I say

I love you, for you are me. You are my Holy Self.

I now open my heart, and let the pure essence of unconditional Love pour out.

I see it as a Golden Light radiating from the centre of my being and I feel its Divine Vibration in and through me, above and below me.

I am one with the Light. I am filled with the Light.

I am illumined by the Light.

I am the Light of the world.

With purpose of mind, I send forth the Light.

I let the radiance go before me to join the other Lights.

I know this is happening all over the world at this moment.

I see the merging lights.

There is now one light.

We are the light of the world.

The one light of love, peace and understanding is moving.

It flows across the face of the earth

Touching and illuminating every soul in the shadow of the illusion.

And where there was darkness, there is now the light of reality.

And the radiance grows, permeating, saturating every form of life.

There is only the vibration of one perfect life now.

All the kingdoms of the earth respond

And the planet is alive with light and love.

There is total oneness, and in this oneness we speak the word.

Let the sense of separation be dissolved.

Let mankind be returned to God kind.

Let peace come forth in every mind.

Let Love flow forth from every heart.

Let forgiveness reign in every soul.

Let understanding be the common bond.

And now from the light of the world the one presence and power of the universe responds.

The activity of God is healing and harmonizing planet earth.

Omnipotence is made manifest.

I am seeing the salvation of the planet before my very eyes as all false beliefs and error patterns are dissolved.

The sense of separation is no more, the healing has taken place, and the world is restored to sanity.

This is the beginning of peace on earth and good will toward all as love flows forth from every heart

Forgiveness reigns in every soul and all hearts and minds are one in perfect understanding.

It is done. And it is so!

John Randolph Price

THE INVOCATION OF THE OMEGA POINT

Know, O universe, that I love you with all the grace, and with all the power of the love of Messiah...*

That my awareness is eternally caressing all forms of reality, sharing this bliss in the most beautiful and creative manifestations...

Let my heart be possessed by the spirit of truth.

Let my existence be dedicated to the enlightenment of all consciousness throughout the universe!

Let my enthusiasm be a light of love and truth for all to feel.

Oh let my touch be the highest manifestation for the will divine.

Let my every action transform this reality into greater and more loving perfections!

Let my body be the most sacred temple of truth!

The omega point is here!

Clarity of vision has been redeemed throughout the universe.

Messiah means 'Self' as we are each a Messiah in our own right. This invocation was given to Robert Coon by the elders of the Melchizedek priesthood in 1975.

THE CATHAR PROPHECY OF 1244 CE

The last of the Cathars were burned by the Inquisition of the Roman Catholic Church at Montsegur, Languedoc, France in 1244. They, however, left this prophecy: In 1986 the church of love would be proclaimed:

It has no fabric, only understanding.

It has no membership, save those who know they belong.

It has no rivals, because it is non-competitive.

It has no ambition, it seeks only to serve.

It knows no boundaries for nationalisms are unloving.

It is not of itself because it seeks to enrich all groups and religions.

It acknowledges all great teachers of all the ages who have shown the truth of love.

Those who participate, practice the truth of love in all their beings.

There is no walk of life or nationality that is a barrier. Those who are, know.

It seeks not to teach but to be and, by being, enrich.

It recognizes the whole planet as a being of which we are a part.

It recognizes that the time has come for the supreme transmutation, the ultimate alchemical act of conscious change of the ego into a voluntary return to the whole.

It does not proclaim itself with a loud voice but in the subtle realms of loving.

It salutes all those in the past who have blazed the path but have paid the price.

It admits no hierarchy or structure, for no-one is greater than another.

Its members shall know each other by their deeds and being and by their eyes and by no other outward sign save the fraternal embrace.

Each one will dedicate their life to the silent loving of their neighbour and environment and the planet, while carrying out their task, however exalted or humble.

It recognizes the supremacy of the great idea which may only be accomplished if the human race practices the supremacy of love.

It has no reward to offer either here or in the hereafter save that of the ineffable joy of being and loving.

Each shall seek to advance the cause of understanding, doing good, by stealth and teaching only by example.

They shall heal their neighbour, their community and our planet.

They shall know no fear and feel no shame and their witness shall prevail over all odds.

It has no secret, no Arcanum, no initiation save that of true understanding of the power of love and that, if we want it to be so, the world will change but only if we change ourselves first.

ALL THOSE WHO BELONG, BELONG;

THEY BELONG TO THE CHURCH OF LOVE.

Acknowledgement to the Fountain Group, U.K.

THE CATHAR MANTRAM

I am the fountain of Light
I am the Truth
I am all Consciousness
I am all Being
I am the spirit of Love, deep unconditional and forever
My gift to the light which is around me is the spark of life
I carry it freely, generously, in purity of the soul
And thus it shall be for ever and ever.

LOVE

There is no difficulty that enough love will not conquer;
No disease that enough love will not heal;
No door that enough love will not open;
No gulf that enough love will not bridge;
No wall that enough love will not throw down;
No sin that enough love will not redeem;
It makes no difference how deeply seated may be the trouble;
How hopeless the outlook;
How muddled the tangle;
How great the mistake;
A sufficient realization of love will dissolve it all.

If only you could love enough you would be the happiest and most powerful being in the world.

Emmet Fox

AFFIRMATION OF THE DISCIPLE

I am a point of light within a greater Light.

I am a strand of loving energy within the stream of Love Divine.

I am a Temple of the Sacred Golden Flame, focused within the fiery will of God.

And thus, I stand.

I am a way by which men may achieve.

I am a source of strength, enabling them to stand.

I am a beam of golden Light, shining upon their way.

And thus, I stand.

And standing thus, revolve

And tread this way the ways of men

And know the ways of God.

And thus I stand.

26

THE BIG SHIFT

he Winter Solstice 2012 was a huge turning point for humanity and the planet. This date marked the ending of many earth calendar cycles. Several cycles all lined up in completion on that day including a 5,126 year long calendar cycle and a 26,000 year Kali Yuga cycle. It was also prophesized to be the ending of time in the Mayan Calendar. Ancient cultures such as the Incas, Egyptians, Maya and Hopi understood the Great Central Sun (the sun behind the sun) is a great portal which directs energy from the Galactic Centre of our Milky Way Galaxy. This day also marked an alignment of the Sun with the centre of the Milky Way Band and the energy streaming from this portal. This means we also have moved into the Galactic Photon Belt which means a greater amount of light is now reaching us. This is what is triggering a massive global spiritual awakening. In this awakening not only is our consciousness being raised, but our bodies are undergoing an immense transformation as well. We are shifting from carbon based cells to that of a crystalline nature that is non-polar. This cellular shift will assist us in letting go of duality, dual based thinking and what we perceive as limitations. The Winter Solstice which happened on December 21, 2012, was the marker for all of this. The changing of the earth's magnetic grid, which started in 1987, now has shifted into being a grid of crystalline nature by 2012. The opening of this crystalline grid is what started allowing emerging vibrational changes in civilization to start taking place as well as the changes in our own body's grid system. We are transitioning from the 3rd dimensional reality to the 5th dimension which some have referred to as Heaven on Earth. Everyone on some level is aware of this shift although for most people it is completely unconscious. They may just feel a restlessness or uncertainty about things they can't put their finger on. This is a time of major shift in our lives, and that of the planet, as everything is vibrationally shifting now. As this upshift accelerates, everything that is not in a similar vibration is being exposed. We see this every day in the world as all the negativity is surfacing. Things are not getting worse on the planet, as some may think, but the negativity which has always been there, is now finally being fully revealed. We see this coming out with the increasing incidents of abuse, gun violence, corruption, and manipulation which is being brought to the surface in full view. This lower frequency energy, wherever it is operating; in institutions, governments, churches, organizations or individuals expressing itself through controlling behaviours, abuse, greed and other practices, cannot stay hidden any longer. With the advent of the five years of transparency, it is all coming to light. The negativity is being revealed so it can be dealt with and released. With the Winter Solstice of 2012, we have now entered into beginning times of a new Earth. The crystalline grid of the Earth is opening up all its stored information to be made available to us. We are being asked to connect with the consciousness of nature and the earth so as to have our lives completely supported. We are experiencing planetary changes, changes within humanity, and changes within ourselves. The children born since 2000 are one of the reasons we, as humanity, are moving forward because they are wired differently. They exist on, and emit, a different frequency than the rest of us. Their frequency is more in alignment to where we are going, rather than the old paradigm of where we have been. We, ourselves, are being asked to become aware that we are now living in an upshift of new energy which is bleeding in. It is important to become aware of these new energies which are impacting us as well as the many tools available to us for raising our consciousness and awareness so as to be in alignment with these new energies. We may find our ways of being, thinking, and operating in the old paradigm just aren't working anymore. The solution to this is to awaken to our spiritual nature, raising our consciousness, and lifting ourselves above the vibration of the perceived problems and challenges in our lives. It is also to get educated about things so we have greater awareness about ourselves and our environment. We've had changes in our food such as the introduction of GMOs which are not compatible with our changing DNA. We are being asked to listen to our bodies and feel what they need. Life is a journey of healing and transformation. As we listen to our bodies, it is possible to work with our cells to be in tune with our environment. We need to train our mind, however, to allow healing to happen.

If fear controls you, you cannot expand. If you allow the light to shine in your life, you will burn through it. When you are in perfect alignment with your spiritual nature, there are no problems. Life is a journey of awareness, we are spiritual being having a spiritual experience in a human body/environment. Each day, as we take the steps that support us, we move forward in ascension. Our higher self has memory of all our lifetimes, all that we have ever been, done, or experienced. In this ascension process our higher self becomes us as we come to understand that the Divine Creator is within us and our connection to nature. There is unity in all things, because how I treat you, is a reflection of me. I am constantly feeling my vibration. It is important to remember, you are a spiritual being, working to not get hung up in the mental body by overthinking things which cause stress and headaches. It is to let go, and to let the Divine within you handle it. We are part of the collective. As we move forward, we come to understand our Avatar consciousness, our Unity Consciousness, our Unified or Christ Consciousness. With this awareness we become an observer, a witness to life without judgment, detached in a way. This is how we awaken the power and awareness within ourselves for we are emerging out of duality. It is for us to remember that we are spiritual beings, having a spiritual experience, in a human body. We are temples of Divine Love emanating a vibration and a frequency. So now, as of 2013, we moved into a whole new place vibrationally and energetically with the energy of Awakened Consciousness beginning to take us into the fifth dimension. Each winter solstice would still bring new energies for the following year, but in addition to that, with this higher energy in place, new openings were revealed. There is now an opportunity for each of us, and for all of humanity, to engage in the 13 steps to bring our lives into further alignment in conjunction with the thirteen inter-dimensional vibrational vortex gateways our planet is going through at the same time. These thirteen steps for humanity and the inter-dimensional Gateways are taking place between the years of 2013 to 2024. This is taking both us, and the planet, along the path of awakened consciousness. I started becoming aware of this process when I was told that, each year, I would be made aware of when, and where, the next interdimensional gateway would be opened with the theme for that coming year. The thirteenth step, and last step, would open on the Winter Solstice of 2023 and this gateway will take us into a year of peace, love and abundance in 2024. Then in 2025 it will be the once in one hundred year conclave of the Great White Brotherhood of Light to determine, at this meeting, if it is time yet to make a decision about the master's reappearance, when they will physically walk amongst humanity.

27

THE SEVEN RAYS

For those of us awakening to this understanding, there are several tools and processes which have been given to us to aid us in making this transition into the 5th dimension. The most powerful ones I have found that work in tandem with the 13 steps, are the Seven Rays and the Golden Flame. As of 2013 the Seven Rays have been awakening us, more and more, to their presence and function in this vibrationally changing world as we climb the ladder of Ascension. Winter Solstice 2012 brought us to a new place of being, with a big shift to the fifth dimension. At this time, it became important for us to begin to understand the universe, how it is organized, and how it effects our lives. To understand this, we must move forward to an understanding of the Seven Great Cosmic Planes. The Universe and the solar systems, within the Universe, exists in an orderly, numerical system of defined graded frequencies called Planes and Sub-planes. Each plane is a level of consciousness and life measured through vibration and frequency. Each plane has seven divisions called sub-planes. All of Life has evolved through the Seven Great Cosmic Planes and sub-planes in a process called involution or evolution. The Seven Rays are a stream of energy that is filtered down to earth and humanity through the big dipper from the great central sun. They carry vibration and streams of colour (think of a rainbow). The seven great cosmic beings (life forms) which we give the name "Lord of the Ray' to, create a frequency or stream of energy/consciousness through their Divine intention, will and purpose. They are beyond our comprehension. They ask us to open our minds and embrace their wisdom, within, so that we can see, without hindrance, the true nature of reality, letting go of the illusion of fear, which holds us back. They create and sustain energies of all that is, as well as that of the Destroyer when evolutionary change is needing to occur. As their frequencies radiate out into our world, the impacting energies produce changes, progress and unfoldment for the new dispensation to spring forth. All that no longer serves humanity, fades away. They create new forms as they are needed which are the building blocks of the new dawn. They also sustain our present forms which are for our highest unfoldment. Their radiating emanations are cyclically brought forth and cyclically withdrawn. The Rays have been operating for thousands of years, but with the shift into the 5th dimension, it is the beginning of a new 26,000 year cycle which is being referred to as the Aquarian Age. All the Rays impact everything on earth, however, different ages are characterized by a certain Ray. RAY VI, which has been in effect for over the last two thousand years, is being withdrawn from dominance in the world right now. It is time to withdraw its energy creating the end days, the end of time, which we are experiencing right now as the old system of being no longer working. Because the dominance of Ray VI is being withdrawn now, people are experiencing the end times. There is chaos and fear as people, particularly the people in power, do not want to change or let go of preconceived ideas of how they think the world needs to be to serve their own interests. We are now beginning to experiencing the dawn of RAY VII which is blossoming forth with its new vibrations, and new ideas. The millennium children and the crystalline children are claiming their power telling the world that the establishment's way of being, and doing things, is not how they want to live their lives. With the dominance of Ray VI being withdrawn, the result has been an increasing cessation and dying out of old forms, institutions, businesses, and ways of governing which do not serve humanity. This is happening in order to make room for the new forms and new life expressions the incoming Ray VII will help create which are the Builders of the new dawn. We are watching the old die away, brick by brick, as we embrace the new concepts and ideas coming forth. The Seven Rays are powerfully intense emanations of light and energy that need to be modulated before reaching earth. They stream from the seven stars of the Great Bear/Big Dipper constellation which are major transmitting agents of the Seven Rays to earth. Each RAY transmits its energies filtering it through 3 Constellations of the Zodiac to our Sun. From the Sun these Seven Rays are transmitted through the seven sacred planets of our Solar System; Mercury, Venus, Mars, Jupiter, Saturn, Uranus, Neptune, and Pluto to further mitigate the intensity of the energy of these rays so they can effectively be received and

The Big Dipper

utilized on Earth. Each Ray has attributes of a colour, stemming from the white light of Source, the heart of God, as it descends into manifestation. Each Ray has a specific area of focus, a cosmic being associated with it, and is embodied by an Ascended Master who is the Chohan of that Ray. These Rays, and the Ascended Masters associated with them, help us become aware of the seven paths back to God as each of these Masters have already walked and mastered this path. It is also through them, that the energy of the Christ and God, filters down to mankind. The Rays are as follows:

RAY I – RED

The Magnificent great being who embodies Ray I is called The Lord of Will and Power or The Lord of the Red Ray, embodied through Master El Moyra. This is a Being/Entity that Wills to

226

Love and uses Power as an expression of Divine Love, Divine Good (the will to do good). It uses the expression of Divine Love to destroy outmoded forms so new ones can be created, ones which will 'continue to reveal God's power and beauty'. Ray I embodies the 'dynamic idea of God' and it is very focused.

Ray II – Blue

The great and unspeakable magnificent being who embodies RAY II is called The Lord of Love Wisdom or The Lord of the Blue Ray, embodied through Master Kuthumi. This is the embodiment of Pure Love which instils into all life forms the quality of Love. It is the MASTER BUILDER who takes the 'dynamic idea of God' embodied in RAY I and formulates the Plan for implementing it (like an architect's plans). This is the blueprint through which everything flows and grows out of. Ray II is the Master Builder and architect of the new form and new consciousness. We are each the draftsman/woman, through our energy and vibration, helping to create new form within the world.

Ray III – Yellow

This great being is called: The Lord of Abstract Intelligence and Adaptability or The Lord of the Yellow Ray embodied by the Master, Paul, the Venetian. This Ray works in close cooperation with RAY II. This lord constitutes the active building force which starts the building or construction of form which eventually materializes the 'dynamic idea and purpose of God'. Divisions and categories are not separations because all life is ONE. Ray III is the builder who creates and adapts new forms with no fear.

RAY IV – ORANGE

This great being is called: The Lord of Harmony through Conflict or The Lord of the Orange Ray embodied by Master Seraphis Bey. Its function is the creation of Beauty through the interplay of life and form. Based on the design on the Divine Plan, it is essentially a healing Ray which brings all form into perfection through the power of the inner life and soul so that the inner beauty is seen below the surface.

RAY V – GREEN

This being is called: The Lord of Concrete Knowledge and Science or The Lord of the Green Ray embodied by Master Hilarion. This great cosmic being is a pure creative channel for the Divine Will. It is a being of intense spiritual light working through the quality of higher mind. In this fifth Ray, heart and mind eventually come together naturally revealing each other to one another. An example of the functioning of this Ray is thinking with our hearts and loving with our minds.

RAY VI – PURPLE

This being is The Lord of Devotion and Idealism or The Lord of the Purple Ray embodied through Master Jesus. This great being expresses a militant focus upon an ideal, a one-pointed devotion to an intent with Divine Sincerity. In a peculiar way, it is an expression of the quality of our solar deity, the Sun god, and a true and vital expression of Divine Nature. Most people in the world are still living their lives ruled by Ray VI, with fanatical religious beliefs filling people with fear. People who express intolerance for anyone else's belief, other than their own, are expressing devotion to a one-pointed fanatical belief.

RAY VII – INDIGO

This being is The Lord of Ceremonial Order or Magic or The Lord of the Indigo Ray embodied by Master St. Germain. Ray VII is the Ray now coming in as the overall influence in our time. It is the new dispensation of the second coming of Christ flaming within us. It embodies the light of the Golden Flame of Illumination now awakening and transforming each of us into beings of Unified Consciousness. The Unified Consciousness is where the feminine and masculine within, are in perfect balance in each of us, also known as Christ Consciousness or the Divine Feminine Consciousness. This Lord builds through the power of thought and makes a person delight in all things done decently, and in order. Mother Mary and Mary Magdalene are very active in this Ray. The Rays help us to master certain qualities and awareness within ourselves so we can ultimately experience our journey through life from the perspective of our Divine beingness, or our Higher Self, who is at ONE with all life and form, the Absolute. In Manley P. Hall's mystical poetry we hear the absolute speaking to Himself/Herself:

THE SPACE BORN

I am the Absolute.
I am birthless, deathless, eternal,
The baseless Base of Beginnings,
The sure foundation unmeasured,

The causeless cause of causation,
The living root of illusion.
All these am I, and other things
Unmentioned;
The sum total of reality expressed
In naught;
Unmoved, unquestioned, undefined:
I am omnipotent.
Veiled by the robes of empty space,
I dream
The troubled nightmare of creation's plan,
To wake and find creation's plan dissolved again
In me ...
Of me you little know, and yet
Am I the sum of all that has been, is, or yet to come -
The plan, the planner and the planned —for all in one ...
I am the absolute; I, the one before the beginning ...
The word unspoken is my name;
I am the all-pervading.*
Manley P. Hall

28

THE GOLDEN FLAME

hereas the Rays are potent streams of cosmic energy impacting the earth and all that is upon it, The Golden Flame is the spark of Awakened Consciousness which resides within our hearts. It is our personal touchstone of our own Divinity, within. This Golden Flame awakens us to the knowing that we are spiritual beings, having a spiritual experience, in a human environment. It awakens us to our Divinity and to our Oneness and it resides within the chalice of the heart. Its holy purpose is to awaken us to our full potential and to accepting fully all that we are. The Golden Flame is about shifting us to a higher reality to accepting that the soul and I are one. As it builds momentum within our hearts, the flame carries the highest vibration of divine love. As we acknowledge this spark of fire of the flame within, it opens up our conscious mind to limitless possibilities. It is the flame of our spiritual bonfire, allowing us to pull in all aspects of ourselves, including our shadow, into our heart to be consumed by the flame which carries the highest vibration of love. Just as when you put a log on a fire, it burns to ash and the fire burns bright, so too the Golden Flame burns bright turning to ash all that is no longer serving us. This is the flame of the true essence of our heart. It is Golden like the Sun, it illuminates wisdom and love through understanding, perception, discernment, precipitation and comprehension. The Golden Flame represents Love, Wisdom and Illumination. It beats within our heart helping to instigate the movement of our evolution and the raising of our frequency and awareness that we are Divine Beings. It asks us to go within, and connect, with the architect of our life stream to rediscover the joy of living our life according to our own unique pathway, and the divine essence, of our heart. This divine essence is the true Source of all that we are, and can be. It takes us more fully into the fifth dimension. It is bringing us the energies of the new dispensation of the Aquarian Age. As we reclaim our Divinity, it beats within the pathway of our heart. As we fully embrace and trust this Golden Flame, we evolve allowing new ideas and connections to pop in. It triggers growth so that miracles can happen when we surrender, as the flame of love transmutes everything. Connecting with the Golden Flame of Illumination the Golden Flame resides within the chalice of our heart. Within this chalice is a pink rose. Out of the beauty of the rose, flows the golden flame. As this flame permeates through the cells of our body, we are transformed. We can visualize this flame reaching upward to our high heart, traveling out the throat chakra, moving upwards to our third eye and then on to our crown chakra, illuminating our divine vibrational connection to the cosmos. The frequency and vibrations we put out, is what we will receive

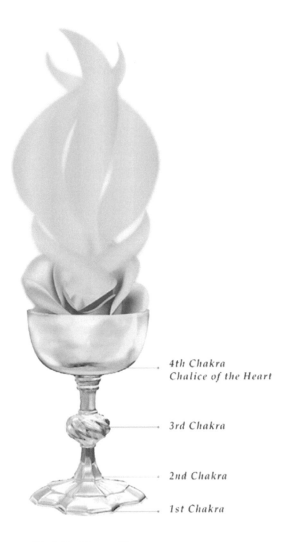

4th Chakra
Chalice of the Heart

3rd Chakra

2nd Chakra

1st Chakra

The Golden Flame of Illumination

233

back in some form whether it be love, compassion, gratitude, forgiveness, or joy.

ORIGIN OF THE GOLDEN FLAME OF ILLUMINATION
The Golden Flame has remained dormant for thousands of years. With the advent of the Winter Solstice, 2012 and our shift into the 5th dimension, the energy of the Golden Flame was awakened. It is a flame of Love, Illumination and Wisdom. It is associated with the Ray II of Love-Wisdom. It is the flame that is the energy/vibration behind the 13 steps which coincide with the 13 gateways that humanity and our planet are now going through. This culminates with the 13th step at Winter Solstice, 2023 with 2024 being the transition year before we move into a glorious new phase in 2025. At Winter Solstice, 2018, another aspect of the flame was made known, that of Illumination making it now the flame of love, wisdom, and illumination. When we connect with the flame, it emanates illumination out into the Cosmos through our crown chakra.

ATTRIBUTES OF THE GOLDEN FLAME ARE:
We are each born with the seed of the Golden Flame within our hearts.

The Golden Flames embraces the heart of all mankind.

The Golden Flame reminds us that we are divine spiritual beings, having a spiritual experience, in a human body.

The Golden Flame of Illumination awakens us to ancient wisdom and our own Divinity.

The Golden Flame is the flame of Illumination, Love, Wisdom, Knowledge, and Peace. It is the flame of Ascension.

It is for each of us to acknowledge that this seed, this Golden Flame of Illumination, is the seed of our Divinity and resides within each of us. It is about love, equality and perception.

The Golden Flame is the totality of our consciousness as we set our intention to reawaken all the attributes of our consciousness—our Unified consciousness—our Christ consciousness. It is the Flame of momentum of movement, the flame of the second coming.

THE THREEFOLD GOLDEN FLAME

There is also a threefold aspect of the Golden Flame which connects with us at the Solstices and Equinoxes. The Solstices and Equinoxes are a time of major shifts in our world and our planet. The Threefold Golden Flame is connected with three locations on our planet all connected by the same ley line. Tara in Ireland representing Love, the Great Pyramid in Giza representing Wisdom, and Lake Titicaca on the border between Peru and Bolivia representing Illumination. During the solstices and equinoxes, we do a Threefold Golden Flame meditation connecting these three major power points in the world which are vortexes/gateways through which the vibrations of the new dispensation flows freely. I have been telling people for fifteen years now that I believe the new dispensation will flow out of Ireland because of it pure energy and its Virgo Soul. Ireland has advanced etheric schools of ancient wisdom opening up now over its sacred sites, especially over Tara. Tara along with the Boyne Valley is the centre of the Golden Crystalline Grid within the land of Ireland. It is the home of the Mother Goddess and the connecting web of ancient temples and stone circles within the golden crystalline grid which now emanates golden flame/light frequencies out into the world. Tara was, at one time, the seat of the High Kings of Ireland and the home of the Druids.

AFFIRMATION OF THE DISCIPLE

I am a point of light within a greater Light.

I am a strand of loving energy within the stream of Love Divine.

I am a Temple of the Sacred Golden Flame, focused within the fiery Will of God.

And thus, I stand.

I am a way by which men may achieve.

I am a source of strength, enabling them to stand.

I am a beam of Golden light, shining upon their way.

And thus, I stand.

And standing thus, revolve

And tread this way the ways of men

And know the ways of God.

And Thus I stand.

236

29

THE 13 GATEWAYS

There are 13 evolutionary steps which humanity and the planet will go through as we shift in consciousness. Starting in 2008 we were being prepared through the five years of transparency for the 13 gateways. The 13 Gateways started with the energy coming in on the Winter Solstice of 2012 setting the theme for the year 2013. The energy coming in on the Winter Solstice of each year shifts humanity, while the opening of each of the 13 Inter-dimensional Gateways are energetic streams of energy which shifts the planet. The opening of the first Inter-dimensional Gateway took place on the Spring Equinox of 2013 with the final step taking place on the Winter Solstice 2023, taking us into the mystical year of 2024. The final opening and streaming of energies of the 13th Gateway with be a shift for humanity, and an interplanetary shift for the planet, as both will be happening at the same time, unlike all the other Gateways. This will be a huge shift in consciousness as 13 is the number of transformation. It is in the year 2025 when it will be determined; if and when, the Masters will start walking amongst us again as we fully enter the Aquarian Age. The Gateways are very special times when the cosmic energies are intensified. In a sense, each gateway and place of opening, offers the opportunity to get turbo-charged and propelled into our next level of consciousness and evolution. As we climb Jacob's ladder, or the stairs of Ascension (Self-Realization), we come into more alignment and resonance with the Avatars, Masters, Saints, Sages and Beings of Light who have walked this journey ahead of us. As we go through these steps, we need to be aware of the power of sound in our lives and of which sound can either can help, or hinder. The vibration we put out either helps or hinders because our voices carry a frequency. The use of our voice and sound is an important ascension tool. In this evolutionary process, it is vital to become aware of our speech, being mindful of the sounds and vibrations of our voice. Our voices carry vibrational energy which can be uplifting and positive, or limiting and negative. Each word we utter, depending on its tone, has a vibration. This vibration can be of love, or destruction, depending on the context we use it in. If it is voiced in anger, it can have a devastating effect not only on ourselves, but on those who are on the receiving end of it. Gossip is another challenge because of the destruction and devastation that is puts forth through the spoken word. Gossip and spewing forth communication from lower states of consciousness, opens us up to negativity and lowers our vibration. Gossip creates separateness, not oneness. As we climb the ladder of ascension we need to be consciously aware of our words and the vibrations they carry. It behoves us to consciously choose our words and tone carefully to ensure they carry forth higher vibration. We also are being encouraged to become aware of, and to let go of, using words such as: try, should, have to, never, good and bad. These words not only carry certain lower vibrations, but also keep us rooted in duality when our intention now, is to rise into unity. In alignment with this holy purpose, I was asked by Spirit to bring a group of participants to the Isle of Iona in Scotland for five days, commencing one day before the Spring Equinox in 2013. This was so we could perform a special ceremony for opening the First Gateway, whose energy had been building since the Winter Solstice. The theme for the year 2013 was Awakened Consciousness. Twenty-three of us gathered for this special ceremony that can best be described as wondrous. The night before the Spring Equinox, we were told by our hosts on Iona that from 9:00 am until 5:00 pm there would be no electricity on the island as the power station was being shut down for its annual maintenance. We took this as an omen knowing that there would be no electrical current energetic output to disrupt the energies of our ceremony. We gathered in Iona Abbey at 11:00 am and no one else was there. All was very quiet that day because of having no electricity. We were able to perform our ceremony and invocations with peace of mind and great ease and the results were astounding! We opened an interdimensional gateway in which amazing energies were brought through it with the ceremony lasting about ninety minutes. We each experienced extraordinary energies touching and enfolding us. Upon completion of our meditation, we departed the Abbey, deep in thought, feeling supremely blessed by all we had experienced. That night we celebrated and gave thanks for the experience with an Essene Silent Supper. For the next three days we visited the Abbey, each day, where we did meditations, prayer, or some private work. Each morning we had a meeting to share with each other what was happening, as each day we experienced new energies and new awareness about who we were. The transformational process of this inter-dimensional gateway continued within each of us, opening us up to the many gifts of spirit, and bringing us many new experiences as we felt our energies, vibrations and frequencies, shift with the power of this divine initiation. Upon returning home, participants found themselves in a state of greater conscious awareness in their daily lives. The healers, in the group, found that their healing abilities were very much enhanced allowing new insights and understanding to come forth. At the Autumn Equinox 2013, we gathered at Chartres Cathedral in France, where we performed a ceremony in the garden opening the second inter-dimensional gateway, the second one for that year. Words seem inadequate to describe the experience, except to say that the connection we felt with the Cosmos, the other worlds, was profound in this ancient Druidic site upon which the Cathedral had been built. This was a place of sacred connection to the ancient wisdom. As we walked the labyrinth in the Cathedral, we felt energetic changes taking place within, as each one of us moved more deeply inward. That energy stayed with us. As the Winter Solstice of 2013 arrived, we were given the theme for 2014, awakening to the Soul's Journey which brought about a lot of questions. As we journeyed within, listening inwardly, we were able to draw more soul awareness and soul purpose into the physical world of matter, helping us realize our reason for being. Although this was often accompanied by chaos and indecision, it was a way of asking us to go deeper to look at our soul's blueprint and the work we agreed to do. It also brought to us the awareness that the soul does not die it only returns to the world of souls to decide on its next quest. The journey of Ascension brings with it the promise, "There is more to life than is revealed. Soul knows life in the subtle worlds". It is in the quest for living this promise that the spark of great creator connects us to the Golden Flame, the fiery mind of God, and the Divine's transformative love. We were asked to take a deep look at ourselves and to let go of what was no longer important in our lives as our soul awakens to the beauty of the, now moment, fulfilled and enlightened. The ceremony for the opening of the Third Gateway was once again at the Abbey on Iona at 5:00 pm on the Autumn Equinox of 2014. Again, we had the Abbey to ourselves. As the group gathered in a circle, we had another experience lasting over ninety-minutes of wonderfully powerful inter-dimensional energy surrounding us. We did our ceremony and invocations, anointing of ourselves and receiving the many blessings being showered upon us. It was so powerful that not everyone was able to stay standing in the circle and they had to sit down instead. This was a wonderful mystical experience as it is, and was, a mystery beyond explanation, a cosmic experience. That evening, just as we had done after the spring equinox Gateway of 2013, we once again celebrated with an Essene Silent Supper. The next day we again visited the Abbey, feeling it vibrations and allowing the effects of the experience to anchor itself deeply within each of us. Next we took a hike, climbing to the highest part of the island, where we performed a water initiation/purification ceremony at the Well of Eternal Youth which blew our socks off. We seemed to have stepped out of time into another dimension being blessed by the gifts of the Mother. In the end, we spent three delightful, awe-inspiring days on the Isle of Iona. The next day we visited the Abbey nunnery, shared our experiences in a workshop, and walked to the beaches where we explored the many sacred points on the island. A few months later, on the Winter Solstice 2014, we were given the theme for 2015 which was to be, awakening to Our Own Divinity. It was apparent that 2015 was going to be about connecting with Spirit and realizing that all we have is NOW. It was going to be about being aware of our Oneness, letting go of the fear and the sense of separateness, which is duality. We were being asked to let go of what holds us back from being our true selves. We needed to allow ourselves to open up to Unity/Unified Consciousness, to allow the Divine Light/Flame to guide us. When we raise our vibrations and raise our consciousness, we speed up our soul's evolution as we climb Jacob's ladder through the pathway of the heart. This awakens us to the fact that love conquers all and that fear causes separation. This is how religions controlled us for years. Now that religion's influence is waning, our governments have taken over the role of creating fear to control the masses. We have the unholy trinity (the United States, the United Kingdom and Israel) and their friends who have created a ferocious beast of fear, working to bring about the One World Order and a cashless society where bankers and their associates rule. The time has come when no longer will we have bail-outs for banks, only bail-ins which the depositors will pay for. I already was aware of this

242

before 2014, but put it on the back shelf to look at later. But back to the Gateways. I had had an astounding experience when I first visited the renowned psychic healer and medium, John of God, in Brazil in 2015. Words are not adequate to describe all that happened to me there. The experience at the Casa was life-changing for me. The essence of my being altered as I absorbed the energies of the Casa and the entities, the beings of light there, along with meeting other people involved in the healing work performed in this crystal healing city. My profound experience began on my second day there when I underwent my first Crystal Bed Bath session. In this session I felt the presence of entities such as King Solomon, St. Ignatius of Loyola, Dr Augusto de Almeida, Mary Magdalene, Dr. Valdivino, and Master El Morya who worked with me on all levels in this Crystal Bed Bath session and other healing sessions. This was a spiritual adventure in which I had to allow myself to be completely open to healing all aspects of my life. I was forever changed by this experience. I became aware of, and felt, as if I was journeying through this mystical pathway during my time there. At a soul level, it was similar to what I felt, and lived through, during my first visit to India. I was so affected and transformed by the time I spent at the Casa, I now offer spiritual journeys to Brazil so others can have the experience at the Casa as well. I know there is a lot of controversy surrounding the arrest of John of God, but in my experiences at the Casa I never heard anyone ever share anything that was questionable about his nature. The profound and potent energy remains at the Casa even if John of God is physically there or not. I do know my experiences there over a number of years were so profound, on all levels that after my first time there, I scheduled a subsequent series of two-week personal retreats at the Casa for July 2016 and 2017. This seemed fitting because the year 2015 was all about being aware of our Oneness. You can only do that when you are whole within yourself. To become that Oneness takes healing and forgiveness on all levels of one's being. For the Fourth Gateway ceremony, we gathered in Ireland. This was held at Tara, the seat of the High Kings and Druids of Ireland. Tara is a mystical place, not only in Ireland, but also in the larger cosmic scheme of things. This is because it is a sacred site where the light is anchored for the emerging new consciousness. Once again, we opened another interdimensional gateway which allowed the energies of the second coming to stream forth. As this energy poured forth, it touched us all; lifting us, the site of Tara, and all of Ireland to a new level of being. This was appropriate since Tara is an ancient mystical site. With all it mysticism and the fact that Ireland, itself, is known as the island of saints and scholars, it is fitting that this interdimensional Fourth Gateway opened up here. Ireland and especially, Tara, was and is, a University of Light whose ancient books are stored in the etheric plane here. In past times, Ireland's Universities of Light stored the ancient wisdom throughout the dark ages. One of the Emerald Tablets is even buried on the grounds of Tara. Tara was a place which once had connections to the Phoenicians and the Atlantians as well as serving as the centre point of the Three-Fold Golden Flame. At Tara, as our group gathered in a circle, we could all feel the shift in energy not only within ourselves, but also in the land. This was a shift in conscious awareness for each of us as we felt the etheric download of the

Fourth Gateway take place. We left Tara humbled by our wonderful experience, ready for our next step. I was then informed that the opening of the Fifth Gateway would take place back on the isle of Iona in Scotland so we went back there for the Autumn Equinox of 2016.

AUTUMN EQUINOX OF 2016

The year 2016 was all about Awakening to Clarity—by moving through our shadow! We live in amazing times. The Universe seems to be bending over backwards to help us become spiritual beings capable of being clear expressions for the Divine. Much healing work has to be done on the emotional and mental bodies to achieve that goal. We also have a physical body, which naturally accompanies us on that journey. I found out, through my own experiences and my own body, how important it is when one is on a spiritual journey, to have a body free from pain. To do this we must listen to what our body is telling us. The Awakening to the Soul's Journey which commenced in 2014, brought us many challenges. It asked us to look at our lives and to consciously work on ourselves. This process gave birth to the energy of 2015, which brought us an infusion of Divine Light. That infusion has moved Humanity and the Earth into higher frequencies of consciousness; conscious awareness, energy, and vibration. We are all now feeling the impulse of the Second Coming within, the energy of the Universal Christ Consciousness or Unified Consciousness. Some people resist the term Universal Christ Consciousness because they feel it is based in Christianity, but that is not true. Universal Christ Consciousness is the level of enlightenment we were bathed in

at the time of our inception, the moment we were first breathed
forth from the Core of Creation by Infinite Spirit/our Father-
Mother God, the great creator. As Sons and Daughters of
Infinite Spirit/Father-Mother God, Unified Consciousness,
Universal Christ Consciousness, and the Divine Feminine is the
level of enlightenment we must ALL return to if we are going
to continue our evolutionary process; to walk through the eye
of the needle, so to speak. Our return to Unified/Christ
Consciousness will be accomplished by healing ourselves,
releasing the programming we received as children, and in our
society, which has adversely effected our lives. By doing so, with
greater awareness we can return to the Path of Divine Love and
Ascend up the Spiral of Evolution (Jacob's ladder) to the next
level of our awakened consciousness, awareness and learning
experiences. If, however, the term Christ Consciousness prevents
you from hearing the message being given to us at this Cosmic
Time, then by all means change that term to whatever resonates
with you as whatever other name you want to use for God;
Source, Reality, Infinite Spirit, Universal Consciousness, Unity
Consciousness or whatever else you feel content with as there is
no one 'right' name, you choose. Please, however, allow the
Cosmic Opportunity of the added Light in the year of 2015,
which is an '8' year, to be received within your being. This
expansion of Light creates a sacred space so that our heavenly
guides and angels are able to encode the energies of the Fifth-
Dimension, the Crystalline Frequencies of Divine Love, to all
life forms on Earth. This frequency connects us with The Beings
of Light in the Realms of Illumined Truth. You may begin to
be aware you may have had connections, or experiences with

beings that have taken you to another level of evolutionary awareness, thus climbing Jacob's ladder. These experiences can happen in the dream state, in meditations, or even during quiet moments of reflection. We are ONE. There is NO separation. Consequently, when large numbers of people focus their attention on a particular event, such as a Group Meditation with a stated purpose, a collective Cauldron/Chalice of Consciousness is formed which can influence the entire planet. In order for that to happen, we simply need to focus and resolve that we are coming together for a Holy Cosmic purpose as we invoke energy to be used for the highest good of all concerned, in the fulfilment of God's Divine Plan. I believe that the seed of Universal Christ Consciousness was brought to earth by Master Jesus. Mary Magdalene representing the soul of that consciousness. It was 'She' who grounded it on earth. We are now birthing that consciousness as we return to the path of Divine Love, the second coming, which is taking place within each one of us. Look at certain days of the year where love is flowing in abundance: Valentine's Day, Mother's Day, Father's Day, and Christmas Day. These days are all about the birthing of love, honouring the role played by both the Masculine and Feminine aspects of love. Winter Solstice, 2015, brought us to Awakening to Clarity, the theme for 2016. In the year 2016, we were being asked to look deeply at our shadow aspects (the negative, fragmented aspects, undesirable aspects of ourselves which we want to hide from others). We were now being asked to acknowledge what we saw as our shadow aspects as they were being revealed. We were shown that we needed to recognize that this shadow aspect exists within each of us, as well as within each institution, organization, and company; and within each country. Once we comprehend the shadow and embrace it, it offers us soul growth and expansion to be open to our gifts we may not have known were there, or do not yet understand. As we are brought face -to- face with our shadow, we have now reached a point in consciousness where we can no longer continue to sweep things under the carpet. Anything we do not want to acknowledge, or we resist; the energies which started in 2015 are forcing us to look at it. If we are unwilling to look at our shadow aspects, we will continue to have chaos in our life. The shadow wears many faces; fear, greed, anger, vindictiveness, selfishness, manipulation, victimization, co-dependency, laziness, control, hostility, ugliness, and anything that is weak or judgmental. The list goes on. Our shadow/dark side acts as a storehouse for all unacceptable aspects of ourselves—all the things we pretend not to be, all the aspects of ourselves that embarrass us or we would not want to have mirrored back to us. Even though we may not want it, this mirror is held offering us opportunities to look at ourselves through our daily encounters. Each person, or situation, that causes us discomfort is a mirror for us. It is for each of us to embrace our shadow, and befriend it, so we can move forward embracing all aspect of ourselves into unity, within. Along with the shadow work, spiritual and physical ascension also included is the releasing and clearing of old energy patterns of dis-ease and limitation which affect us physically, mentally, emotionally, and spiritually. These old energy patterns hold us back from being able to express our magnificence and the true potential of our soul. It is not only emotional karmic clearing we are being asked to do, but also clearing of the energy distortions which affect the physical body. The path to enlightenment is not only about the search for Divine Light, but also the acceptance of the shadow self within ourselves personally and the shadow playing out in the world. In 2016 we had a front row seat seeing the shadow of America play itself out. This was evident in the presidential election when Donald Trump totally demolished the Republican Party by breaking up the old paradigm as they were no longer being of service to the people, or humanity. Now for the Republicans to move forward in these new energies, they must look at what they stand for and how they are going to serve the people. This will not be a quick fix as there are too many Republicans still entrenched in the old ways of doing things. It will take some chaos for them to come to the realization that the game has changed. Now, in this new energy, it is about doing the right thing for humanity, for the country and its citizens whom they represent. Gone are the days when our public representatives represent only the big multinationals like big pharma, banking, insurance, oil and chemical companies to the determent of the people they are supposed to represent. Now the Democrats are no different than the Republicans. They too have not been of service to humanity. Hillary Clinton, all on her own, brought down the Democratic Party as they lost touch with their grass roots and the people they represented. Both parties received a message from Middle America, the forgotten and the disenfranchised, telling their representatives that they were no longer willing to be lied to, or be forgotten at the behest of the people who rule through fear and intimidation using perceived threats and creeping fascism. Politics became the tool of big conglomerates so they could take over the world using imperialistic tactics introduced to America during the Bush/Cheney era as they, in effect, shredded the constitution and the civil rights of the American people.

The path of love is about reclaiming our vulnerability. It is about expressing our own unique gifts, talents, and the deep desire to love ourselves so we come to understand and embrace who we are. It is not an easy path to love what we have hated, to love what we feared, and to love what has haunted, or hurt, us. It is often easier to hold on to the pain of the past rather than moving forward into the healing of this moment. It takes courage, will and belief to heal the challenges which confront us. In confronting these challenges, we find forgiveness, healing and love. Winter Solstice 2016 brought us the theme for the year 2017, Awakening to Wisdom. Here we are being asked to look at our belief systems, to see and comprehend what we understand about wisdom. It was time to become aware of what we believe. It is through our belief systems that are often evident through what we say and think, that we shape our life and our manifestations. This is an essential truth of the Law of Attraction as each thought we have, has a frequency/vibration. It is for each of us to become the gatekeepers of our own thoughts. Even though our thoughts have frequency and vibrations, it is not so much our thoughts, as much as the underlying belief systems which generates our reality. If one believes they are poor, then they will always be scraping to make ends meet. Your belief creates that experience. If one believes that they are not smart, and they've taken on that belief, they limit themselves, their experiences and achievements in life.

We are constantly projecting our beliefs out into the world. Like a boomerang, then the manifestations of our beliefs returns to meet us face-to-face. We forget we are having a physical experience in order to learn the lesson that our beliefs translate into feelings, thoughts and emotions which ultimately causes our experiences in life. We can, however, change our beliefs and experiences through conscious awareness and doing the inner work on ourselves. 2017 brought us the theme of Awakening to Wisdom. This sixth step for humanity was again brought forth at Tara in Ireland, which was also the location of the Fourth Gateway. The Sixth Gateway was to navigate and awaken to wisdom and all of the many gifts, wisdom bring to us. The sixth inter-dimensional Gateway was opened at Tara at Autumn Equinox. Again we are reminded Tara was the ancient seat of the High Kings of Ireland and seat of the Druids. As we ceremonially opened the Sixth Inter-Dimensional Gateway, Tara's Etheric Libraries of Light were now available to us. With the opening of this sixth inter-dimensional Gateway we were more acutely aware of how these Inter-dimensional Gateways were being orchestrated and overseen by Mother Mary, the Masters, Avatars and Beings of Light. From the opening of the very first Inter-dimensional gateway, these beings have been orchestrating everything as well as overseeing the downloading of ancient knowledge and the new knowledge as we walk through the thirteen steps of ascension. With this gateway awakening to wisdom, it also helps us better understand the ancient teachings of the seven rays which brings us insights to what is happening in the world today. It is another part of ourselves we are meant to reclaim in order to remember who we really are. The

WISDOM is within. All of us desire greater wisdom as we quest our path each day. We come to understand even though we may be looking, we do not always see, or understand, the whole picture. It all depends on our perspective and point of view. If, for example, you see a burning building and if you were looking at the fire from the east side, you get a certain perspective. If you were looking at it from the north side you would get a different perspective. But if you were in a helicopter, overhead, you'd get a bird's eye view seeing the whole area. When we can approach our lives with the whole range of emotions and an overall perspective that is wisdom. What do you see? What do you comprehend? In embracing it, even if you do not fully understand it, you will grow in awareness and understanding even if you do not fully comprehend it. When you embrace a concept, which you do not fully comprehend, you are taken to another level of understanding. A new understanding bleeds through into your consciousness as wisdom.

All of us carry a desire for greater wisdom and understanding than that which we currently possess. Seek and you will find, as it is there, hidden within us. Sadly this is often the last place we look because it takes work on our part. Most of us are so busy looking outside of ourselves for the quick fix, when all the while, it is within us. It was there all along in our consciousness which is the divine interface between God and us, as mortal beings. The subconscious mind is the God part of us, that part of our amazing self that contains all the knowledge and wisdom of 'all that is'. Our unconscious mind contains the soul's memory, journey and all of the records of our lifetimes stored as a great mega computer, within us, also known as the Akashic Records.

The goal of achieving spiritual growth is through walking the pathway of the heart, crossing the threshold into the sacred garden of wisdom, where all can be embraced and filled with compassion, love and joy. Religion is about binding us back to God through dogma. Spirituality is about tending that Golden Flame which burns within each of us. Life is a wonderful gift especially at this time of major shifts and transformation for humanity as we embrace the new Age of Aquarius, the water bearer. We are here to experience how to fully embrace the Now, the Oneness, the beauty, and the transformation that surrounds us without judgment. The more we can stand outside the box, just observing, using our discernment without emotion or attachment to the outcome, this is what enables us to fully embrace the Oneness. We are the builders of the new dawn, the building blocks which anchor the way forward as the vibration of the second coming takes place within each of us. As the builders of the new dawn we understand we are co-creators with Source, with the Cosmos. We hold the power to command the universe, which is within ourselves.

Winter Solstice 2017 brought us the theme for the year 2018, awakening to Beauty. We were being asked again to look and understand what beauty is, and that it is not just, skin deep! There is beauty in nature, in buildings, in objects, in animals, in humans, in flowers, gardens, in the wilderness, rivers, mountains, and in everything if we have the eyes to see it. Beauty is about love seeing and being present in the now. Quite often we miss beauty because we do not take the time to look, and feel, the essence of beauty. Here again, we are being asked to look within. We must unwrap the package to see what is inside. There is an old saying, 'never judge a book by the cover', and so it is with beauty. Beauty asks us to take all we have learned about wisdom within ourselves and apply it to beauty. In awakening to beauty, we awaken to the beauty within ourselves, to aspects of ourselves which we have not seen, nor understood before because we have been conditioned to always look outside of ourselves for beauty; when truly, beauty is within.

2018 brought us the seventh step for humanity to experience as we ascend along the pathway/vibration of ascension. It leads us to the seventh inter-dimensional gateway which was opened at Chartres Cathedral on Spring Equinox 2018. Chartres Cathedral was built upon an ancient Druid oracle site with its seven streams of consciousness and like Tara, it was also the seat of an ancient mystery school. Again, there is much ancient wisdom stored here in the Etheric Libraries of Light which are now also open. Opening the Seventh Inter-Dimensional Gateway at Chartres on the Spring Equinox helped to bring forth the plan for humanity, the creation of Oneness consciousness. This was especially needed in this time of post denominational living where religion has lost its pulse because it was based on a state religion, which put the need of the institution, before the needs of the people. Winter Solstice 2018 brought us the theme for the year 2019, Awakening to Strength. This theme is asking us to be aware of what strength means in our lives as well as the vibration and energy it carries. Strength is about balance and power in our lives. It is inner strength and power which allows us to stay focused on our daily practice and our pathway of the heart. This strength also helps us not to get caught up in drama and our emotions. As we utilize our inner strength, bringing forth discernment, we can be outside the box of the drama viewing only with love. On Autumn Equinox 2019 we were at Mount Carmel, Israel to open the 8th Gateway for humanity. This inter-dimensional gateway energetically opens us to a new vibrational rate for ourselves and the planet. Strength gives us the power to move with love, joy, forgiveness and compassion as we continue unfolding and remembering who we are. Strength is about forgiving yourself and embracing your shadow bringing you into wholeness. Strength is also about expressing gratitude for ourselves and our life. It allows the Golden Flame of Illumination which resides within the heart, to vibrate out into the world.

Winter Solstice 2019 brought us the theme for the year 2020 of Awakening to Group Consciousness. Here we are being asked to remember our Oneness and to see the beauty within ourselves and others, as we quest each day. It is to continue to experience these vibrational changes within, as we journey along the path of ascension. This is a transitional year, a year when a new world view will emerge in our consciousness. On the Spring Equinox of 2020, we will be on the banks of the river Ganges in Varanasi, India to open the 9th Gateway for humanity and our planet. This inter-dimensional gateway energetically opens us to a new world view with a new vibrational rate for ourselves and the planet. Group Consciousness awakens in us the power of group meditation whereby when we, as a group, envision and move energetically with love, joy, forgiveness, and compassion the group consciousness greatly amplifies and magnifies this process so we begin to remember who we are, not only individually, but start to wake up, collectively. Group Consciousness is about us being builders of the new dawn, as representatives of the emerging new Earth. The new dispensation coming forth, and the receiving of the energies of the Aquarian age filtering through into our lives, provides for greater ease of allowing the Golden Flame of Illumination within us to vibrate more powerfully out into the world. Winter Solstice 2020 will bring us Awakening to Empowerment for the year 2021. Here we are being asked to recognize that we are divine beings, temples of divine love and it is up to each of us to acknowledge that we are divine beings of light and love. It is for us to embrace our limitless divine potential, to nurture ourselves by putting ourselves first in love, understanding, gratitude and compassion. When we are empowered there is no fear because I and my soul are one and above all else I am both will and fixed design. Empowerment is a power pack of energy which brings us total freedom of mind, body and spirit, it is the pathway of the heart. Empowerment the 10th inter-dimensional gateway will open at autumn equinox on the Isle of Iona. Winter Solstice 2021 will bring us Awakening to Balance and the 11th inter-dimensional gateway will open at the Sphinx on spring equinox 2022. I await the themes for 2023 and '24 as this process continues up to Winter Solstice 2023. At that time the final message will be given for the year 2024 preparing us to move into the very special year of 2025, when the once in a hundred year conclave of the Great White Brotherhood meets again.

SEIZE EACH MOMENT!

As we quest on our journey, each day, the forward movement of this process is to look at what we need to embrace or change in our life. But at times, we all procrastinate despite our so called good intentions. In the past I have been a great procrastinator in letting go of certain issues or in working on forgiveness for issues from the past. But now I have come to understand, that the longer I take to do this inner work, the only person I am hurting is myself. So I realize now I need to get on with it as soon as possible. However, I still have one challenge that I have not yet overcome, and that is packing. I have spent many a night without going to bed when I am heading out on a tour early next morning to catch a flight. At about 10:00 pm I will get around to getting my packing done and printing off all that I need for the trip. I have still not resolved this challenge, but I plan to. So that which we do not face, or embrace, and that which we do not resolve; can, at any time, resurface for us to look at. It will continue to pop up sometimes at the most inconvenient times. It pops up at these times to get our attention until we make a decision to sit down to do the inner work to resolve it. Relying on our wisdom is essential in utilizing our time here in this dualistic world as it requires us to genuinely express self-love valuing ourselves in all that we do each day. Procrastination and laziness are our greatest obstacles. If we keep putting things off until tomorrow, what we forget is that, tomorrow never comes. As we travel the pathway of the heart embodying the golden light, we also attract the shadow, as the deeper parts of ourselves keep being revealed and resolved. The more we ascend Jacob's ladder, the more criticism we may draw about being weird. This is because as our light body changes, it creates discomfort in some people as they no longer resonate with our vibration. They don't know what to talk with us about or how to deal with us as our light body vibration changes and is no longer in sync with their vibratory rate. We are perceived as weird and our thinking is viewed as off the wall, if it does not conform to the norm but who decides what is normal? This requires wisdom to deal with this. It is for each of us to remember who we are. It is for each of us to learn to stand steadfast in our truth. Standing up for our truth is a peaceful action, done in love. It sends attacking energy back to its source without malice and with love.

PRAYER OF PROTECTION

Father-Mother God, I ask that I be cleared & cleansed within the White Christ Light, the Green Healing Light, and the Purple Transmuting Flame.

Within God's Will & for my highest good

I ask that any & all negativity be completely removed from me, encapsulated within the Ultraviolet Light and cut off from me.

Impersonally, with neither love nor hate,

I return all negativity to its source of emanation decreeing that it not be allowed to re-establish itself within me, or anyone else in any form.

Now I ask that I be placed within a capsule

The White Christ Light of Protection, and for this blessing, I give thanks.

So it is!

Our Father Mother, Who is throughout the Universe,

Let Your Name be set apart

Come Your Kingdom

Let your delight be in Earth
As it is throughout the Universe.
Give us bread for our necessities today
And forgive us our offenses as we have forgiven our offenders.
And do not let us enter into materialism
But set us free from error
Because yours is the Kingdom and the Power and the
Song from age to age sealed in faithfulness and truth.
Amen.

As we grow in the wisdom of our conscious awareness, we then can choose to deal with conflict without engaging in it. When we observe it with discernment, from a standpoint of emotional detachment, we find this is the only way to resolve any situation. The law of belief governs what we create in our lives. It is however, much more expansive than just knowing what our beliefs are. It incorporates our perceptions; what we see, what we understand, and the extent to which we are open to changing our opinion and stretching our beliefs. Within our belief is also a contract, which brings us challenges so that we achieve self-growth. So as we grow, we come to understand that, through our wisdom, we let go of old patterns, limiting beliefs, and illusions that have mired us in a never ending repetitive cycle of the old belief system. If we do not learn from our lives past challenges or experiences, we are destined to repeat them until we learn the process of breaking the old cycles through divine inspiration, or divine mind, as we challenge ourselves to break free.

30

MY JOURNEY HOME

As I look back over my life's journey, I now see and understand that I chose all of it. I chose my parents and my path in life. Nothing happened to me which I did not, in some way orchestrate, for advancing my life's purpose. I began to see that the threads of my awakening started with my mystical experiences as an altar boy. I can also see how the 'cracking of ego' occurred through the challenging people and situations in my life, first with my father and then later when I married Bernadette, who was just like my father. I now understand how the continuing pattern of this abuse contributed to my first conscious moment of awakening when my attorney friend Oliver asked me, "Have you ever thought that you are an individual with needs, too?" I had always been so focused on what I needed to do to make others happy so they would be at peace that I never thought about myself. This opened by eyes to a new path, which I took. I am grateful for all my experiences even the ones in jail and in prison in Northern Ireland as they brought me to who I am, and where

I am today. I now know myself to be a spiritual being, having a spiritual experience, in a human body which is living the inner Divine Wisdom. I believe we are living in a magical time of transformation which I am so happy to be part of and I can see and feel myself shifting and changing daily in my vibration, energy and frequency. I greet each day with love and immense gratitude for my 'rebirth' and each morning I awaken with a prayer to the Divine Mother, in thanks, for her guidance. My greatest joy in life is being embraced by the energy of Divine Mother each day, and those of my Avatars and Beings of Light guiding me each day. Each morning I address Divine Mother and Father Mother:

PRAYER TO THE DIVINE MOTHER

To Thee, Oh Divine Mother, I raise my entire being, a vessel empty of self.

Accept, Mother, This is my emptiness and so fill me with

Thy Light, Thy Love, Thy Life,

That these, thy most precious gifts,

May radiate throughout my whole being,

And overflow the chalice of my heart

Into the Hearts of all

Whom I may meet, greet, touch and contact this day

Revealing unto them the joy of thy beauty and wholeness

And the serenity of our divine peace and love, which nothing can destroy.

GOOD MORNING FATHER MOTHER GOD

Dear Father Mother God,

Take me where you want me to go.

Let me meet who you want me to meet.

Tell me what you want me to say.

Let Divine wisdom flow through me.

Let my soul lead the way, and keep me out of your way.

Thy will be done.

Thy will be done.

Thy will be done—and so it is.

I truly believe anyone can heal themselves and release their pain and suffering by listening to their body and taking the necessary steps which allow the universal energies to work with them and support them. There are so many ways of healing which have brought me into more conscious awareness; the Divine Feminine Emotional Healing work which Mother Mary passed along to me, as well as the herbs, vitamins, supplements, and essential oils which evolved into Matrix Nutrients. I know all of these came about because my priority has always been to follow the guidance from my soul as my soul and I are one. Each morning I say:

I Am the Soul

I am the soul of ...

And also love am I

Above all else I am both will and fixed design

My will is now to lift the lower self into the Golden Light Divine

That Light am I

Therefore I must descend to where the lower self awaits
Awaits my coming that which desires to lift and that which
cries for lifting are now at one
Such is my will.

Each morning I look to see what it is I can do to improve my
life, what is it that I need to embrace as I express gratitude and
appreciation for myself, my work, health and the abundant flow
in my life this day and every day. I also work with other
incredible teachers and healers, such as Dr. Sue Morter, whose
amazing techniques of Bio-Energetics, Quantum Science, and
Energy Codes results in increased creativity, health and healing.
My path continues as I do my inner work each day. Using my
daily spiritual practice as a cornerstone of my belief, the second
coming of Christ Consciousness that is taking place within, the
pathway of the heart and the Golden Flame of Illumination are
all leading me on an amazing journey. Evolving along the
pathway to the 13th Gateway, and beyond, I embrace my body
fully, as I awaken each day to new energies, vibrations and
frequencies. Part of my awakening process is for me to integrate
each of these with the spiritual being I AM as I grow in greater
understanding of the Oneness. My message to you, is to
embrace life fully, igniting the vision of living in the Aquarian
age. As I experience the freedom brought to me by embracing
the frequencies, energies and vibrations that guide me, I
encourage you to do so as well for we are all coming home to
the One, the soul of the Unified Self:

Come Home

I am here within.

I am your soul, your friend speaking to you.

I am the soul mate you yearn for.

S/he whom you have been seeking outside of yourself... Is actually deep within.

I am here within you.

Not separate from you, but one with you.

Come Home, Move inward.

For this is where you will meet me.

And all the longings of yesterday will cease to be.

For what you have been seeking has been within you all along.

Author unknown

31

WINTER SOLSTICE 2019
AND INDIA 2020

The Winter Solstice of 2019 brought us the theme for the year 2020 of Awakening to Group Consciousness. Here we are being asked to remember our Oneness, to see the beauty within ourselves and others, as we quest each day. It is to continue to experience these vibrational changes within, as we journey along the path of ascension. This is a transitional year a year when a new world view will emerge in our consciousness. On the Spring Equinox of 2020, we celebrated on a boat on the river Ganges in Varanasi, India to open the 9th Gateway for humanity and our planet. This inter-dimensional gateway energetically opens us to a new world view with a new vibrational rate for ourselves and the planet. Group Consciousness awakens in us the power of group meditation whereby when we, as a group, envision and move energetically with love, joy, forgiveness, and compassion the group consciousness greatly amplifies and magnifies this process so we begin to remember who we are, not only individually, but start to wake up, collectively. Group Consciousness is about us being builders of the new dawn, as representatives of the emerging new Earth. The new dispensation coming forth, and the receiving of the energies of the Aquarian age filtering through into our lives, provides for greater ease of allowing the Golden Flame of Illumination within us to vibrate more powerfully out into the world.

INDIA 2020

Our experience in India on our sacred journey was way beyond anything I had experienced in my previous 12 visits to India. Starting with Darjeeling, Tiger Mountain and our connection to the Temple of Goodwill in the etheric above Darjeeling, we had so many experiences followed by the Taj Mahal, the Jain Temple in Ranakpur, Krishna Temple complex and much more. While on this sacred journey the coronavirus appeared in India and by about March 17th most spiritual tour groups had left India but we continued our journey because when I checked with Mother Mary she told me we were on a Divine Mission and we were fully protected, this I shared with our group who were fully committed to doing the work but we did have one person leave on the 19th as we departed Delhi for Varanasi to find that we were the only group in our hotel just like in Delhi. March 20th Spring Equinox, we are on an early morning boat ride on the river Ganges to experience the amazing sunrise as we watched the golden sun rise above the horizon, shortly thereafter at 6.30am our time we connected with sacred mystical journeys meditation group at 7.00pm Mountain time US on the 19th their time for spring equinox being led by Barbara Poulin a local shaman and a good friend of mine. Our connection was amazing as we did our ceremony and meditation to open the 9th inter dimensional gateway this being a divine mission was being directed by Mother Mary, Master el Morya, along with other beings and Avatars of light. This experience on the boat was vibrationally very moving and energetically transformational and our group had some amazing experiences and shifts take place within, some of which took at least two weeks to process. Now we had a new challenge, all the flights we were originally booked on were cancelled so now we had to re-book with the help of my travel consultant Greg and so we all departed Delhi on the evening of March 21st and early morning on the 22nd for Mexico City via Tokyo and the rest of us to Newark and San Francisco all being on the last flights to leave Delhi for these cities. We now arrive home to a whole new experience with lock down being in place whereby we could go out to walk, to the grocery store and the post office but all restaurants were closed with the exception that you could get take out. A new world, a new environment where we were now on retreat in our homes. We now have choices with what to do, we were given the opportunity to look at our lives especially at our health and food because we know that eating the right food can prevent many diseases such as heart disease, cancer, type 2 diabetes, Alzheimer's, arthritis and many other ailments. This time is asking us to get back to basics, to take time for our spiritual practice of prayer, meditation, chanting, yoga etc. We are to go within and look at ourselves, to take stock, do we love our self, do we express forgiveness, gratitude, appreciation, compassion and loving kindness for ourselves, time to visit with family in your home or visit with family and friends on Skype, Zoom and What's App. All the things we were too busy to do before we had this enforced retreat. Remembering that we are vibrational beings and that just like cell phones and Wi-Fi etc. we emit a vibrational frequency and energy and this can be either positive or negative. We can use our positive energies to take us to a higher vibrational rate and frequency which is above the vibration of the coronavirus and with this vibration we can transmute the virus through our prayer meditation and group meditations. Then on April 7th along came the Full Moon in the zodiac sign of Aries, it is also the first sign of the Zodiac and the full moon of Aries determines Easter as Easter Sunday always falls the Sunday after the full moon. This full moon amplified the energies brought to us at Spring Equinox and that was the energy of transition in this the year of awakening to group consciousness. We are now a world in transition from the Piscean age to the Aquarian age as the doorways to the 3rd and 4th dimensions are now closed, there is no going back and it is up to each of us to embrace the energies, vibrations and frequencies of the 5th dimension remembering that we are spiritual beings having a spiritual experience in a human environment. Aries is the birthplace of ideas, a spiritual impulse taking form. In Aries we plant the seed and sound the many notes of optimism. When these seeds sprout they carry a note, a higher spiritual impulse reminding us that we each carry and emit a vibration, frequency and energy and it is up to each of us to be responsible for taking these vibrations to a higher frequency as we quest the pathway of ascension for ourselves and for the planet. As we become aware and work on our frequency, vibration and energies we lift ourselves and the energies of viruses, as all disease starts in our etheric body and works its way in. What we emit is what we send out and that is the vibration we attract if we send out fear and anxiety that is what we attract back. Think about what you say and the tone you use as that is what you are sending out. Like attracts like just like the hundred monkey syndrome. The coronavirus has brought home to us there is no separation no individual, nation or group no matter what their social standing are immune to the virus. We are a global community inter dependent on one another being asked to look at the consciousness of the Divine Feminine and the Christ consciousness where the feminine and masculine energies within each of us is being brought into perfect balance towards a unified consciousness as we walk the pathway of the heart. This is the pathway to the new dawn, the new dispensation which serves humanity as the old paradigm no longer serves humanity. We are in the frequency of change, of transition as the old boy network falls apart in these end times. Easter represents a major initiation, remember the Easter egg is about renewal and Easter is about Resurrection not about the crucifixion, it is about the magnetic power of will of the Christ to draw all men and women to the indwelling Christ consciousness (Unified consciousness) in every heart out of the world of material values into the spiritual world. It does not relate to death but to life. What is death? There is no such thing as death, just like fear it is an is an illusion as our soul does not die it carries on its mission lifetime after lifetime seeking out new and evolving experiences. Remember we each choose our experiences, we arrive here on earth with a blueprint and that blueprint is completed along with some modifications along the way. The soul chooses to take on these experiences in this lifetime to help with the ascension process before moving on. Remember the soul never dies as I have learned from Mother Mary and you can always talk with another soul whether they be living or in the world of spirit to bring about healing, forgiveness and reconciliation.

Regeneration is happening in nature at this time, be open to allowing it to happen to you. There is nothing to fear but fear itself. Trust in yourself, trust in the divine within you, and trust that you are a temple of Divine Love and of the Golden Flame of Illumination. We have spent the last 2000 years in gestation, now we are bringing forth the birth of the new dispensation, the second coming is happening it is happening within each of us whereby we take back our power from the church and government which we had given it away to and they have abused that privilege. The coronavirus has awakened us to reclaiming ourselves as we each have the ability under our retreat conditions to go within and discover our true selves. Easter is a time of resurrection (3 days in the tomb), it is a microcosm of our current lock down. How are we preparing for resurrecting ourselves during our time in the tomb! A time of birthing just like the seed of the Christ Consciousness was birthed at the time of the resurrection and Mary Magdalene became the soul of that consciousness. We are now the seeds/draftsmen/women being initiated into the Second Ray of love and wisdom bringing forth the new plan for humanity as all that does not serve humanity falls away. This is a time when we are being baptized into group consciousness just like Jesus was in the river Jordan to allow the Holy Spirit/ the Christ energies to work through him during his three year ministry. We are now in a time when we ourselves and the planet are letting go of the coarser frequencies of the status quo and start to rise up from the tomb of materialism through raising our vibration. It is a time to face the daemon on the threshold—our shadow and to review that which we have swept under the carpet and that now needs redeeming and embracing within our self. The great combined influence of Jesus and the Christ was Triumph over death...by misusing the significance of this great event, much external fear has been created by the church/government and materialistic forces and this theme of emotional fear is now being used in this era of coronavirus so much so that it has generated a fear that is itself the real Virus. We are each a field of energy, vibration and frequency, with the true capacity to recreate ourselves as we come to love ourselves enough to embrace our own power. We are beings of pure light, temples of divine love emitting a frequency and a vibration out into the world, a world of which we are the creator. We are re-birthed each day to begin again walking the pathway of the heart, discovering and embracing who we are.

APPENDIX

SACRED MYSTICAL JOURNEYS

Your life is a spiritual journey, with divine spiritual inspiration, emanating within each one of us. We desire to keep growing, to be our best selves, to stay profoundly connected to our planet, all beings, and engage in our fascination with uncovering the mysteries of our natural world and her sacred places. At Sacred Mystical Journeys, we travel to ancient sites which still carry the imprint of the ancient spiritual wisdom. Together, in search of spiritual adventure and transformation, we visit stone circles, healing wells, sacred mountains and modern crop circles. We explore pilgrimage routes and ancient paths, connecting with these sacred energies wherever we go. We are walking the path of the mystics. As we tour, I share my knowledge of the mysteries of these sacred places and the traditions that the people practiced, this connects us to the sacred energies of the sites and provides messages from spirit for us. During sacred travel, you may feel a certain connection with the Gods, Goddesses, Druids, Fairies, Saints and others beings of light who have come before us. Inspiring and empowering transformational spiritual journeys for the body, mind, and spirit, walking the path of the mystics. On our sacred tours, you are being asked to feed your soul through meditation, sacred ceremonies, rituals, healing and sound healing to enhance the awakening to the many wonders of the miraculous and the mystical energies at these sacred sites.

www.sacredmysticaljourneys.com

MOTHER MARY

Mother Mary is my constant companion. I receive divine inspiration and divine guidance from her each day as I continue my spiritual quest and follow my path in the world. This has been ongoing since my initial experience with her in May 1990, to all of the times and ways she has chosen to give me messages and communicate with me about different issues over the years. When she has something important to impart to me, she takes a seat in the back of my car and talks with me while I drive. She has talked to me about many things like instructing me to create Divine Feminine Conferences, or issues pertaining to people who are being bullied or maligned online when she asked me to come to that person's defence in bringing the issue to a close. She also gives me messages for people about certain situations that are happening, or that are about to happen. Her messages are all about bringing balance, wisdom and power to their lives or my life so that they or I can look at issues with detachment and discernment. Her focus with me, right now, is to be at peace, to be aware of how sound, vibration, energy and frequency are impacting, and being impacted by, the different energy shifts happening on our planet and in our lives. She asks that we open our hearts to who we are and express gratitude for who we are,

273

temples of divine golden light emanating pure golden light out into the world. We are being asked to love ourselves, as love is the most powerful tonic in the world as it emanates out from our hearts. The frequency is Divine Love.

You are ONE. We are ONE. We are ONE.

MARY NETWORK HEALING

Mary Network Healing encompasses the Divine Feminine Emotional Healing instructions that were given to me from Mother Mary. This process is all about networking the memory cells of the body to bring about healing on all levels. Mary Network Healing is a technique that results in emotional, physical, mental and spiritual healing. It calls upon the power of the Divine Feminine to extract unresolved pools of emotions and unproductive thought forms. These blocks were created by a person's inability to deal with these emotional traumas at the time they occurred. These blocks often obstruct the flow of energy through the body resulting in physical, mental and emotional pain. The Mary Network healing techniques allow the practitioner to release blocked energy that has been held in the client's body. The practitioner guides the client to release the trauma held in the body's memory cells. Then the practitioner helps the client to rejuvenate these memory cells, filling this void with golden-white light and thus healing takes place within the physical body. This modality also includes soul-to-soul conversations, long distance healing, and past life healing as well as trauma from miscarriages, other life situations, or grief from the loss of a loved one. This healing is offered through individual sessions and there is also a practitioner online training course being developed.

THE AQUARIAN CROSS

The Aquarian Cross symbolizes Sacred Union, a cross of perfect balance of Christ Consciousness. It is an equal-armed and perfectly balanced cross with an open centre incorporating the Golden Mean and Vesica Pisces symbols (two interlocking circles)—the basis for all 'Sacred Geometry'. Additionally, the point of overlap of the two circles represents the pre-Christian symbol of the fish, the vulva or the proverbial 'eye of the needle' through which we must all pass sooner or later in perfect balance, in order to achieve Christ Consciousness, Unity Consciousness. It is perfect balance; it represents the Law of One and the Christ Consciousness—the sacred union of the Masculine and Feminine. The vertical represents the Masculine, the horizontal represents the Feminine. The two interlocking circles represent: Spirit and Matter—Heart and Mind—Christ/Sophia—Masculine and Feminine. When one has the mystical marriage of heart and mind, one walks through the eye of the needle (the little space between the two circles—the Vesica Pisces—the doorway—the fish—the entrance to the womb) into our own Divinity (chalice). It is the universal cross which signals the end of the duality of the Piscean era and heralds the golden age of Aquarius. It is post denominational.

MATRIX NUTRIENTS

The best nutrition for your body is whole food. Matrix Nutrients are, quite simply, food without the bulk. Our vitamins and minerals are truly natural supplements because they are made from real food. The body is able to absorb and use the active nutrients in our products much more efficiently because it is real food. In contrast to other so-called 'natural' supplements, since ours are made from foods, not chemicals, the body recognizes these supplements as foods which are absorbed into the blood stream within twenty minutes of taking them. Their rate of absorption is at minimum, 85%. We believe that the solutions to our health dilemmas have been provided in a natural and unprocessed state by Mother Earth. Using these gifts as they existed for centuries is how to truly heal and honour your body, mind and spirit. Yet, with the degradation to the earth over the years, the ability of Mother Earth to produce healing foods and remedies has been diminished. Therefore we, at Matrix Nutrients, have created a bridge to those natural healing gifts of the earth with the products we provide.

https://matrixnutrients.com

ACKNOWLEDGEMENTS

I wish to thank all of the following for their support, love and inspiration.

Mary Tatone, Robert Gongloff, Julie and Matthew Tierney, Judith Driscoll, Dr. Joe Vaughan, Elizabeth St.Angelo, Austin Delaney, Tracy Johnson, Carol Beyer, Charlene Fleener, Ilene Hill, Lori Napstad, Jim and Patricia Vincent, Noel Ross, Richard and Pamela Skeie, William Ross, Bernard Llewellyn, Carolyn and Allen Otto, Dr. Betty Carper, Sally Brown, Jim McCarthy, Brendan Corballis, Dr. Carol Parrish and numerous others who have helped me on my path.

I also wish to thank my brothers and sisters especially my sister Catherine, and her husband, Con for their amazing support while I was in Northern Ireland. In addition, I want to thank Tom Patton for all his legal assistance in the United States and Joe Rice for his legal assistance in Belfast along with my brilliant senior counsel, Arthur Harvey. Lastly, I want to thank Linda Moise for helping me start this book and Catherine Ann Clemett for her amazing assistance in helping me bring this book of five years in the making to the final furlong.

✿

✫